SCIENCE CRAFTS for KIDS

▲ ▲ ▲

GWEN DIEHN & TERRY KRAUTWURST

This edition published exclusively
for **DISCOVERY TOYS, INC.,** by
Sterling Publishing Co., Inc., New York.

Editor: Carol Taylor
Design: Dana Irwin
Photography: Evan Bracken
Production: Elaine Thompson and Dana Irwin
How-to illustrations: Gwen Diehn
Cartoons: Susan Wood
Watercolor, p. 125: Dana Irwin

10 9 8 7 6 5 4 3 2

A Sterling/Lark Book

Published in 1994 by Sterling Publishing Co., Inc.
387 Park Ave. S., New York, NY 10016

Created and produced by Altamont Press, Inc.
50 College St., Asheville, NC 28801

© 1994, Gwen Diehn and Terry Krautwurst

ISBN 0-8069-0283-3

ACKNOWLEDGMENTS

We'd like to thank the people who contributed to *Science Crafts for Kids* in a variety of ways.

Additional Photography

Racoon, page 18; Spider Web, page 37; and Rainbow, page 131, Bill Lea, Franklin, North Carolina.

Woodhouse Toad, page 25, David M. Dennis, Tom Stack & Assoc.

Archaeologists at Work, page 32, courtesy Dr. Bruce Smith, Department of Anthropology, National Museum of Natural History, Smithsonian Institution, Washington, D.C.

Triceratops, page 34, Smithsonian Institution, Washington, D.C.

Rocks, page 39, courtesy Chimney Rock Park, Chimney Rock, North Carolina.

Space Shuttle, page 59, courtesy NASA.

Airplane in Flight, page 71, courtesy Boeing Airplane Group, Seattle, Washington.

Lightning, page 77, Gary Milburn, Tom Stack & Assoc.

Wave Patterns, page 81, Thomas Kitchin, Tom Stack & Assoc.

Dyeing of Fibers, page 87, courtesy Krantz

Mabry Mill, page 97, courtesy the Blue Ridge Parkway, National Park Service

Freighter, page 109 top, Dana Irwin; Supertanker, page 109 bottom, courtesy *Aramco World*, Houston, Texas

Sun With Solar Flare, page 114, courtesy NASA

Polar Bears, page 119, Anna E. Zuckerman, Tom Stack & Assoc.

Milky Way, page 143, Dr. David Talent, Cerro Tololo Inter-American Observatory, Chile; NOAO photo

General Helpfulness

The Silver Armadillo, Asheville, North Carolina, for lending the pieces of quartz for cover photo and for photo on page 40.

Fran Loges, teacher at Issac Dickson Elementary, for lending her class to make a bird hide.

Chris Ahrens and Solar Box Cookers International, 1724 11th St., Sacramento, CA 95814, for sharing their plans for the solar oven found on page 115.

David, Michael, and Erik Diehn, for project ideas, project testing, and manuscript reading.

Kids

Jaha Avery, Scott Blackwelder, Will Hillier, Jake Palas, Demar Shabazz, Antwan Thomas, Summer Vanselow, Nakesha Wedlaw (bird hide)

Anna and Mary Bracken (centipede kite, solar oven, pit kiln, hot air balloon). Anna: underwater viewer, cross staff.

Susan Britton (mold garden)

Nathaniel Cannon (wormery, rocket kite, waterspout, solar stone)

Allyson Deese (fire clock, gluep)

Mark Eaton de Verges (mill, thunder stick, helicopter, periscope)

Paul Kim (cabbage indicator paper, nephoscope, water lens)

Ginger Kowal (plant tepee)

Jesse Krautwurst (hovercraft, root viewer, astrolabe)

Ben Mackle (wormery, hypsometer, xylophone, rocket kite, marbled paper)

Tristan Mills (centipede, solar oven, pit kiln, hot air balloon)

Austin Sconyers-Snow (sound viewer, clay boats, apple garland)

Mariah Thomas (wind sock, color spinners, science log, wave in a bottle)

Jennifer Wald (clay tiles, centipede kite)

E A R T H

10

A I R

44

CONTENTS

WATER

FIRE

Welcome
to Science Crafts for Kids

EARTH

AIR

When you hear the word *scientist*, what sort of person does your mind's eye see? Is it someone in a lab looking at test tubes full of bubbling chemicals? Somebody studying complicated formulas? A person gazing into a microscope?

Some scientists do those things. Others search for lost cities, record the songs of whales and dolphins, study ancient medicines, look for undiscovered stars and planets, explore deep caverns, track the paths of caribou herds, walk in space, fit together dinosaur skeletons, find cures for diseases, and—well, you get the idea. There are lots of different kinds of scientists! All scientists, though, have one thing in common. They're absolutely, irresistibly, gotta-figure-it-out curious about *how things work and why things happen.*

Does that describe you, too? Do you wonder how the world works? Do you like to learn by *doing* as well as by reading and looking? Great. Then you're really going to enjoy making the crafts in this book.

All of the projects in *Science Crafts for Kids* are fun and interesting and rewarding. Some are simple and will take just a few minutes to complete. Others are more complicated and challenging. But no matter which project you tackle, when you finish you'll have something you can be proud to call your own. And in the making, many of the projects will help you understand important scientific ideas. Others will help you create tools and instruments that you can use to conduct your own scientific studies.

So please: Don't just sit back and read this book. *Use* it. There are a lot of terrific crafts to make in these pages. And there are a lot of eye-opening discoveries to make about this amazing, wonderful world of ours. Let's get started!

A Few Tips About the Crafts Projects
☞ More than 2,000 years ago, Aristotle and other pioneers of science believed that everything in the universe was made up of just four kinds of elements: earth, air, water, and fire. These days,

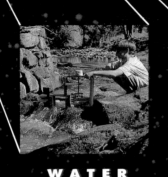

WATER

FIRE

we know better. In honor of the beautiful simplicity of the idea, however, we've organized this book into earth, air, water, and fire sections. Feel free to skip around from section to section and project to project.

☞ Read the instructions all the way through at least once before you begin a project. As you read, imagine yourself actually *doing* each step. If there's something you don't quite understand, ask an adult for assistance. Then go through a trial run with "pretend" materials. You can substitute pieces of scrap paper for pieces of wood, for instance. Acting out the instructions usually makes things clear.

☞ Collect all the materials and tools listed under "What You'll Need" for your project, then start. If you don't have some of the items listed, try to think of things you *do* have that will serve just as well. Be creative! Use your ingenuity!

☞ Several projects involve the use of an electric appliance, such as a hair dryer or hot plate. Others require a sharp knife. Adult assistance is suggested when such items are required. It is always important to be careful and to follow the instructions.

☞ Some of the crafts may call for tools or materials that you've never used or even heard of before. Don't let that stop you! Tools aren't mysterious things used only by adults and unavailable to you. Stores carry them and sell them to people who aren't one bit smarter than you are. People who work there will know what an awl or hacksaw blade is, and will find it for you. After you go look at one, you'll know, too. With the right tool, a job that looks hard (maybe even impossible!) becomes easy.

☞ One notion we want you to get from this book is that science isn't just a subject you learn in a classroom. It's a way of looking at the world. Everything has its own interesting story to tell, of why it is the way it is. As you use this book, think of how the ideas you're reading about apply to the things around you. And never stop asking the most important question in science: *"Why?"*

Science Log

It's helpful to have a notebook to jot down plans, observations, lists of things you need for projects, and other information. This logbook is easy to make, and, because it has a ring binding, you can add pages when you need to. It also has a stiff cover, so you can use it as you would a clipboard when writing outdoors or away from a table.

What You'll Need

2 pieces of cardboard, each 6 by 9 inches

Pieces of leftover wallpaper or wallpaper samples*

White craft glue or rubber cement

A glue brush or an old paint brush

A razor knife

Scissors

About 10 sheets of white typing paper

About 5 sheets of grid paper (optional)

A hole puncher

An awl or a large nail

2 looseleaf rings, either 1- or 1-1/2-inch size

A piece of string about 2 feet long

A pen or pencil

*Paint stores that sell wallpaper will often give you their old sample books if you ask for them. If you can't find any wallpaper, you can use self-adhesive shelf paper instead.

What to Do

1. First make two book covers. To make a cover, lay one piece of 6- by 9-inch cardboard on the wrong side of a piece of wallpaper. Trim the wallpaper so that it is about 1-1/2 inches bigger than the cardboard on all sides.

2. Cover one side of the piece of cardboard with glue. Place the glue side down on the wrong side of the wallpaper, centered so that the 1-1/2-inch border is all around the cardboard. See Figure 1.

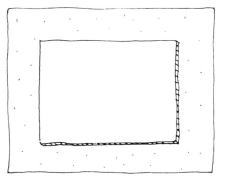

Figure 1

3. Trim each corner. See Figure 2.

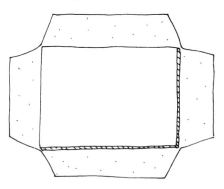

Figure 2

4. Place the cover on the table so that the wallpaper side is down and you can see the cardboard of the book cover. Put glue on each of the four corner flaps, and fold each one up to glue it to the cover. See Figure 3.

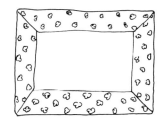

Figure 3

5. Cut a piece of wallpaper to fit 1/4 inch inside the edges of the cover. Glue this endpaper to the inside of the cover so that you can no longer see the cardboard. See Figure 4.

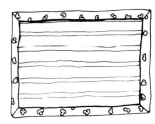

Figure 4

6. Repeat Steps 1 through 5 for the other cover.

7. Cut the pieces of typing paper and graph paper (if you are using it) crosswise in half so that each piece is 5-1/2 by 8-1/2 inches. Stack up the sheets.

8. Punch two holes in the front cover about 1 inch in from each side and about 1/2 inch down from the top edge. You may need to start the holes with the awl and use the tip of the razor knife to widen them if the cardboard and wallpaper are too tough for the hole puncher.

9. Pick up about five sheets of paper and carefully place them under the cover so that they are butted up against the top edge (the edge with the holes) and centered between the side edges. Use the awl or pencil to mark where the holes should be. See Figure 5. Carefully remove the cover, and use the hole puncher to punch two holes through all five sheets at one time. Repeat this step until all of the paper has been punched.

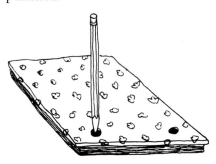

Figure 5

10. Stack up the cover and all of the paper. Arrange it so that the holes are all lined up. Place the stack on top of the other cover. Use the awl or pencil to mark the centers of the holes. Remove the top cover and stack of paper.

11. Use the hole puncher or the awl and razor knife to punch two holes in the bottom cover, where you've marked them.

12. Arrange the stack so that all holes line up. Slip a ring into each hole, and lock each ring closed.

13. Tie one end of the string to one of the rings. Tie the other end of the string around a pen or pencil so that it will be handy when you need to record something.

9

THE EARTH—

where would we be without it?
In this chapter, you can find out a
lot about Earth and its inhabitants.
Build a bird hide and a camou-
flaged periscope to watch the busy
comings and goings of colorful
birds….Grow a mold garden and
watch the "decomposers" at work—
without them, we'd be up to our
ears in all the garbage that ever
existed….Build a home for worms
and one for toads, and watch these
important garden helpers do their
work….Make a root viewer, so you
can see the beginnings of new
life….Craft a handy box for your
rock and mineral collection….Build
a hypsometer to measure the height
of your house and your favorite tree.
And feel closer to Mother Earth
than you ever have before.

EARTH

This little hut will let you get close to birds and small animals without scaring them away. It's easy to build and just as easy to take apart and move to a new location.

What You'll Need

4 strong, straight sticks about 4-1/2 feet long and 2 inches in diameter

6 lighter (but still strong) straight sticks about 2-1/2 feet long

2 forked sticks at least 2 feet long before the fork

100 feet of strong rope

Scissors

A small saw or strong branch cutters

An old sheet or bedspread from a double bed, preferably green or brown

Small leafy branches

What to Do

1. Lay two of the large sticks on the ground side by side and as far apart as the length of two of the smaller branches. Lash the smaller branches between the two large sticks, using about 6 feet of rope for each lashing. See Figure 1 and detail of Figure 1.

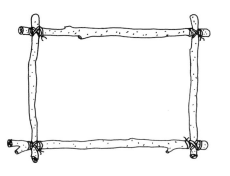

Figure 1

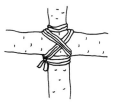

Detail of Figure 1

2. Do the same thing with the other two large sticks and two smaller sticks.

3. Ask a friend to help you hold the two stick frames up so that they're as far apart at the bottom as the length of the remaining smaller sticks. Tilt the two frames toward each other to form a tent shape.

4. Lash the two remaining straight sticks to the frames at the bottom. Lash the two frames together at the top.

5. Use the two forked sticks to make the structure sturdy. First saw or clip off the forks so that the forks are only 2 inches long. Leave the straight ends long. Lash one fork against one of the tilted strong sticks on each side of the frame. Be sure that the forked sticks are on opposite ends of the frame and opposite sides from each other. See Figure 2.

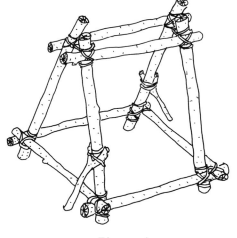

Figure 2

6. Drape the old sheet or bed-spread over the frame. Feel

where the ends of the sticks are, and cut small slits in the cloth so that the stick ends poke out and anchor the cloth at the top as well as the bottom of the frame. See Figure 3.

7. Cut short slits to hold leafy branches in spots all over the cloth, and poke small branches through.

8. Cut viewing holes in the cloth at your eye level on the two large sides of the bird hide. Make the holes about 2 by 6 inches.

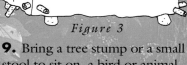

Figure 3

9. Bring a tree stump or a small stool to sit on, a bird or animal identification book, binoculars, and your notebook and pencil when you go bird or animal watching. It's also a good idea to pack some water and a snack!

Whatta-buncha-*ologies!*

The word *science* comes from the Latin word for "knowledge." That makes sense, because scientists are always trying to learn more—to gain knowledge—about our world and universe.

But there are lots of different kinds, or branches, of science. (There's a lot to learn about our world and universe!) What to call them all?

In 1594, Otto Casmann, a European scholar, called the study of humans *anthropology*. The ending came from the Greek word for discussion: *logos*. It was the first time anyone had ever used "ology" (AHL-uh-gee) to refer to science. But it sure wasn't the last. People have been tacking "ology" onto the names of branches of science ever since.

Here's a list of just a few. How many of the sciences can you guess without looking at the right column?

Hint: As hard as some of these look to pronounce, you'll usually be right if you put the emphasis on the OL in "ology"—for example, for *pomology*, the study of fruit, say "po-MAHL-uh-gee."

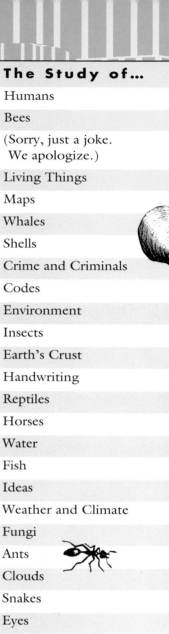

Science	The Study of...
Anthropology	Humans
Apiology	Bees
Apology	(Sorry, just a joke. We apologize.)
Biology	Living Things
Cartology	Maps
Cetology	Whales
Conchology	Shells
Criminology	Crime and Criminals
Cryptology	Codes
Ecology	Environment
Entomology	Insects
Geology	Earth's Crust
Graphology	Handwriting
Herpetology	Reptiles
Hippology	Horses
Hydrology	Water
Ichthyology	Fish
Ideology	Ideas
Meteorology	Weather and Climate
Mycology	Fungi
Myrmecology	Ants
Nephology	Clouds
Ophiology	Snakes
Ophthalmology	Eyes
Ornithology	Birds
Otology	Ears
Paleontology	Fossilized Life Forms
Pedology	Children
Psychology	Mind and Behavior
Pyrology	Fire
Seismology	Earthquakes and Tremors
Sociology	Human Society
Speleology	Caves
Storiology	Legends and Folk Tales
Vulcanology	Volcanoes
Zoology	Animals

Camouflaged Periscope

With this device you can look around corners and spy on birds and small animals without scaring them away. Keep your periscope with you in your bird hide (see page 12) to extend the range of your eyes.

What You'll Need

A long, thin cardboard box, about 20 by 3 by 3 inches

Plastic package tape

A razor knife

2 pieces of cardboard as wide as the inside width of the box and 3 times as long

2 small mirrors, about 2 by 2 inches

Super glue

Acrylic paint

A paint brush

What to Do

1. Tape both ends of the box closed.

2. Lay the box on one of its long sides, and cut a square hole at one end. The hole should be as long as it is wide. See Figure 1.

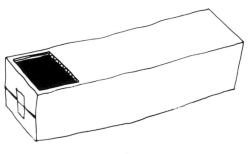

Figure 1

3. Turn the box over, and cut the same size hole at the opposite end of the box, on the opposite side.

4. Fold the two pieces of cardboard into right triangles. See Figure 2. Tape the triangles closed.

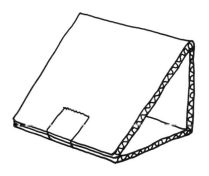

Figure 2

5. Glue a mirror to the slanted side of each cardboard triangle. See Figure 3.

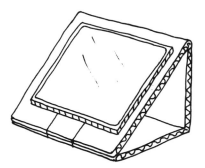

Figure 3

6. After the glued mirrors are completely dry, glue the triangular mirror bases inside the holes in the box. The mirrors must face outward. Wedge the right-angled sides against the back and ends of the box. See Figure 4.

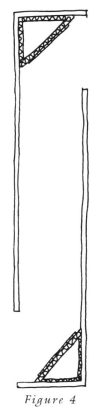

Figure 4

7. With acrylic paints, paint leaf shapes on all sides of the periscope. If the mirrors are in plastic frames, paint the frames, too.

8. To use the periscope, hide behind a tree, a bush, or a fence, and hold the periscope so that one of its openings sticks out so the creature you want to watch is in your line of vision. Look in the other opening. Move the periscope to bring various creatures into your line of vision. You can also stick the periscope out of the opening of your bird hide to extend the range of your eyes.

Camo Creatures *and How to Be One*

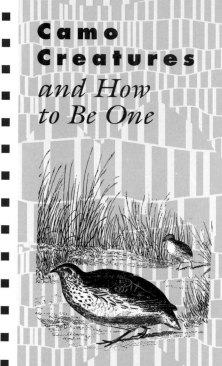

Almost all birds and animals use camouflage—hide-and-seek tricks—to avoid danger or to help them sneak up on a meal without being seen. By understanding the ways nature's creatures hide, you can become a really good hider, too.

Have you ever seen a silhouette, or shadow picture, of a famous person or of someone you know? You can tell who it is just by the shape.

It's the same way in nature. Many birds and animals can't see colors at all—only shades of light and dark. But all wild creatures recognize shapes. If you're a bird, bug, or animal, it's your outline that makes you stand out.

That's why many living things have outline-hiding

"camo" clothes.) Also, remember that your eyes have a telltale round shape. Break up their outline by drawing a stripe or two next to each eye or from temple to temple—like a raccoon's striped "mask." Use a piece of charcoal to do the makeup. (Don't get the charcoal *in* your eyes, though!)

Another kind of natural camouflage is called *countershading*. Have you noticed that many birds and animals are dark-colored on top and light below? Squirrels, sparrows, lions, fish, whales, dogs, and cats (to name just a few) have lighter-colored stomachs than backs. That makes them much harder to see from a distance. Why? Because sunlight from above lightens the dark upper surface and shadows the under surface. So the two shades blend to make a single, less noticeable, neutral color.

Neutralizing your skin color will also help hide you (even if you have dark skin). Rub a light coating of dirt, clay, or dust on your hands, neck, and face to take the sun's "shine" off.

camouflage. They're covered with distracting patterns—spots, stripes, and other designs that "break up" their actual shape. Scientists call this trick *disruptive coloration*. The eye tends to see different patterns on an object as completely separate parts. When an animal is marked with lines and patterns that lead off into the lines and patterns of its surroundings, its outline "disappears." A spotted fawn

resting in leafy sunlight looks like a bunch of brownish plants. A zebra's stripes "scatter" the animal's outline into nearby trees and brush.

When observing nature, you can use disruptive coloration to hide *your* outline. Wear patterned clothing, such as plaid, in shades similar to the surroundings. (Outdoor and military stores also sell specially patterned

Also, remember that animals are aware of shadows and of any movement. When a squirrel hides on a tree limb or when a lion stalks prey, it hunkers down as low as possible to keep its shadow small, and stays absolutely still. Do the same when *you're* trying to be "invisible," and chances are you'll get a better, closer-than-ever look at the birds, animals, and other creatures sharing your world.

Mold Garden

The adults in your house are not going to like this project as much as you will. You may even have to guard it to make sure no one tries to throw it out with the garbage. If you explain that you are studying tiny organisms called molds, you might convince them to leave your project alone. But whatever you do, don't take the cover off of your mold garden when you're showing it to them!

What You'll Need

A plastic, aluminum, or ceramic container at least 2 inches deep and 6 inches square

A trowel or a large spoon

A few trowels of rich garden soil or compost

Orange peels, bread, cheese, and any other foods that you might have seen growing interesting-looking furry coats in the past (except meats)

A spray bottle full of water or a watering can

Plastic wrap to cover the container completely

A large rubber band or string to fit around the container

A magnifying glass

Tweezers

A piece of white paper

A piece of black paper

What to Do

1. Fill the pan about 1 inch deep with soil or compost.

2. Lay the orange peels, bread, cheese, and other foods on top of the soil. You might consider placing them in some kind of design if you want a really handsome garden.

3. Lightly water the garden.

4. Cover the garden with plastic wrap. Hold the wrap firmly in place with the rubber band or string.

5. Put the garden in a warm, dark place. After a day or two, check on it. Continue to watch the garden for changes. If nothing happens after a few days, give it some more water. Make sure the plastic wrap is completely sealed. Put the garden back in the warm dark.

6. When the garden blooms, carefully remove the cover. Be prepared for a smell! Use tweezers to pick up small bits of the mold. Put light mold down on the black paper and dark mold on the white paper. Use the magnifying glass to get a better look at your mold.

7. When you're finished with the mold garden, throw it into a compost heap or bury it in the garden. Throw away the plastic wrap and rubber band. You can wash and reuse the container.

The Fungus *Among Us*

What's black and yellow and orange and brown and red and white and green and blue...gobbles up anything in its path except metal...and lives everywhere—in the air, inside animals, on plants, underneath the ground, in your shoes, and even (eck!) in your ears and mouth? You guessed it: the fungus among us.

There are more fungi (pronounced FUNJ-eye) in our world than any other kind of plant. The mold that grows on food, the yeast that's used to make bread, and the mushrooms that pop up on your lawn are only a few of more than 100,000 different types of fungi. The soil in a small garden contains at least 10 times as many fungi as there are people on Earth!

Most plants make their own food, but fungi can't. So instead they eat other plants and animals—just like people do. The difference is, we eat our food first and then digest it. Fungi do the opposite. They give off chemicals that turn their meal-to-be (a nice fresh banana, for instance) into yucky mush. Then they suck up the liquid.

Their odd eating habits make fungi both friends and foes to us human types. For one thing, we have to go to a lot of trouble to keep fungi from eating our food before we do. Refrigerators help, because most kinds of fungi prefer warm surroundings. But even in cold temperatures hungry fungi will eventually turn the good, solid food *we* like into the nasty, oozy stuff *they* like.

Fungi also make it tough for people to grow food. Most of the plant diseases that give farmers and gardeners trouble are actually hungry fungi digesting roots, leaves, and stems. Even your feet are a treat to certain kinds of fungi that cause the itchy-skin disease known as athlete's foot.

On the other hand, if it weren't for fungi, we'd all be up to our necks in dead plants and animals. Fungi break down, or decompose, plant and animal remains and turn them into plant food and soil. Molds also help us make such foods as cheese and vinegar. And the green mold that you've probably seen growing on oranges or other fruit? That's the famous fungus *Penicillium*. Revolting as it may look, that mold provides us with penicillin, which has probably saved more human (and animal) lives than any other medicine in history.

Plus, we humans turn the tables on at least some of the fungus among us and eat them. Every year we gobble up millions of pounds of mushrooms grown on underground "farms" in caves and old mines.

Some ants are fungus farmers, too. Workers carry bits of leaves into the nest, where smaller ants chew them up and add them to the fungus garden. The insects tend their crop constantly, weeding out any foreign fungi and harvesting the kind they like to eat.

Fuzzy Wuzzy Was a... *Worm?*

You don't usually think of an earthworm as fuzzy, but if you rub your fingers very lightly from back to front along a night crawler's sides, you can just barely feel tiny hairs (called *setae*). There are eight hairs on each ring, or segment, of the worm's body. Earthworms have muscles that can tilt the bristles forward or back, like the oars on a rowboat. They use the hairs to help them move ahead or backward. They also use the hairs to grab onto the soil. That's why it's so hard to pull an earthworm out of its burrow!

A Wormery

The design of this wormery makes it easy for you to trace the tunnels of the residents and observe each day's new diggings.

What You'll Need

A piece of 1 by 2 lumber 22 inches long

A saw

A ruler

A pencil

Sandpaper

Acrylic paints

A brush

Wood glue

2 pieces of plexiglass each 5 by 7 inches

Super glue

A brace and bit, or a hand drill and a small drill bit

4 narrow screws between 3/8 and 1/2 inch long and slightly wider than the drill bit

A screwdriver to fit the screws

Silver or colored duct tape

Black puffy paint (optional)

A trowel or a large spoon

Sand

Dark garden soil or compost

Leaf mold

Cellophane tape

Sheets of tracing paper

A soft, dark cloth about 2 by 2 feet

What to Do

1. Saw the lumber into three pieces. Two of them should be 7 inches long, and the third should be 5-7/8 inches long.

2. Sand the three pieces of lumber.

3. Use wood glue to glue the two 7-inch pieces of wood to the ends of the shorter pieces of wood.

4. When the glue is dry, paint all surfaces of the wood with acrylic paints.

5. When the paint is dry, lay the U-shaped form down flat, and super glue one of the pieces of plexiglass to the top surface. The plexiglass edges should overlap the wood on three sides by about 1/2 inch.

6. When the glue is dry, turn the wormery over and glue the other piece of plexiglass to the other side in the same manner.

7. To reinforce the glue, drill a starter hole halfway down each side about 1/4 inch in from the edge of the plexiglass.

8. Put a screw in each hole. Tighten it down with the screwdriver. Turn the wormery over and repeat Steps 7 and 8 on the other side.

9. Put duct tape along all the edges where plexiglass and wood come together. Use scissors or a razor knife to help with this job. If you want to decorate the wormery, now's the time to draw puffy paint worms crawling along the edges.

10. Fill the wormery with layers of sand and soil. Make each layer about an inch deep. Place a few earthworms below the final layer. Top off the layers with a layer of leaf mold. Lightly sprinkle the layers with water.

11. Cover the wormery with the dark cloth when you aren't observing it.

12. To check and record the progress of the worms, tape a piece of tracing paper to one side of the wormery each day, and trace the layers and tunnels. Put a date on each piece of paper so that you can keep track of the papers and compare the changes that take place from day to day.

13. After a week or so, dump the entire contents of the wormery out into the garden or compost heap and start over. Worms are happier in the earth than in a wormery!

24

A toad is a gardener's friend because it eats a *lot* of insects. Toads like to live in dark, cool holes or hollows in rocks or under debris. You can invite a toad to live in your garden by making a toad house.

What You'll Need

A medium-sized clay flower pot

Acrylic paints

A paint brush

A trowel

What to Do

1. Wash and dry the pot if it has been used.

2. Paint leaf and flower shapes in greens, browns, and other earth colors all over the outside of the pot, including the bottom.

3. When the paint is completely dry, go outside to the garden and find a sheltered spot among your plants. Lay the pot on its side. Use the trowel to bury it halfway beneath the soil. Put some dead leaves and other garden debris in the bottom of the toad house. Check back after a few days to see if any of the debris has been moved. If you're patient, you may catch a glimpse of your toad sometime. If no toad seems to come to your toad house, try moving it to another location.

Toad-ally Awesome

Next time you see a toad, pick it up and get better acquainted. No, you *won't* catch warts. You'd better be gentle, though, or your hand will get slimed.

See those ugly oval lumps behind the toad's eyes? Those are called *parotoid glands.* When a toad is roughly handled, those glands (and others on its skin, including those warty bumps) give off a gooey liquid. The stuff won't hurt your skin. But it does burn and irritate sensitive membranes—like the ones inside an animal's mouth. That's why dogs, cats, and most other creatures that try snacking on a toad spit it out fast. Pretty good self-defense, for a little guy with pop eyes and webbed feet!

Some people confuse frogs and toads, but they're really quite different. Frogs have long legs and smooth, shiny bodies. Toads have short back legs and wide, bumpy, dull bodies.

Frogs are nervous and—well, jumpy. To get somewhere, they leap. Toads are more relaxed and slow-moving. They'll hop if they have to, but they'd rather walk.

Frogs live in and around water. Toads spend most of their time on land.

Also, toads are smarter than frogs. In laboratory experiments, scientists have found that toads can figure out mazes much more quickly than their frog relatives.

Most people think toads are homely but still lovable. To an insect, though, a toad is Godzilla. Do you know how many beetles, grubs, and other bugs an average toad snaps up during the summer? About 110 a day, or roughly 3,300 a month!

To invite a toad into your garden, give it a cool, shady place to live (like the flowerpot toad house on the opposite page). Toads drink by sitting in water and soaking the liquid through their skin. So put a shallow pan of "drinking" water nearby, somewhere private and out of view. And to *really* pamper your pet, put a battery-operated night light near its home, to attract moths and other tasty toad snacks.

Root Viewer

What goes on in the dark under the soil, when the first roots of a baby plant are bursting out of the seed and uncoiling, reaching and stretching and searching for food? This special planter will give you a front-row seat for one of nature's great performances.

Figure 1

What You'll Need

A 1-quart, square-bottomed, plastic freezer container

A sharp knife or razor knife

A piece of plexiglass 5 by 7 inches

Plastic tape 1 inch wide

A piece of black paper the same size as the plexiglass

Cellophane tape

A handful of small stones or broken clay flowerpot pieces

Potting soil

A few beans or other seeds

What to Do

1. Carefully cut from a top corner of the plastic container straight down to the middle of the bottom of the same side. See Figure 1.

2. Make the same kind of cut on the opposite side of the container. Now make a straight cut across the bottom. Remove the cutout piece of plastic.

3. Using the plastic tape, tape the piece of plexiglass to the open side of the container. Be sure that all edges are completely covered with tape and that there are no holes or gaps between the container and the plexiglass.

4. With cellophane tape, tape the piece of black paper to the top edge of the plexiglass so that it can be lifted and lowered.

5. Place the stones in the bottom of the container to improve drainage. Add potting soil to fill the rest of the container. Push a few seeds into the soil about 1/2 inch back from the plexiglass edge.

6. Flip the black paper down. If necessary, tape the bottom edge so that it stays down. Water the seeds, and place the container in a dark spot until the seeds sprout. After they have begun to grow, place the container in the light, and lift up the black paper every day or so to check on the roots. In a few days you should be able to see them and watch their progress. Since roots tend to grow straight down, the slanted, clear side of this container should make the roots clearly visible.

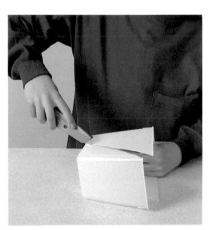

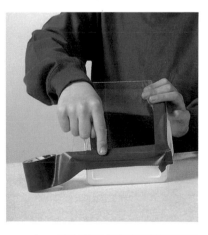

Seed Cast Tiles

When you walk through the woods or across a field in autumn, you'll find pods and other seed heads with interesting shapes. Clay casts are a nice way of collecting these intricate and beautiful objects.

What You'll Need

Low-fire potter's clay*

A rolling pin

Dried seed heads from plants

A table knife

A paper clip for each tile

A board about 1 by 3 feet

White conte crayon** or white chalk

Acrylic matte medium**

A soft paint brush

*Clay can be bought in a craft supply store.

**Both conte crayons and acrylic medium are available from an art or craft supply store.

What to Do

1. Before making the tiles, you need to wedge the clay—that is, get rid of air bubbles that could cause the tiles to break in the kiln. To wedge the clay, pound and knead it for about 10 minutes.

2. Roll the clay out to a 1/4-inch thickness.

3. Cut the slab into rectangles or squares the size that you want the finished tiles to be.

4. With your fingers, press a seed head into each tile. If the seed head is prickly, wear garden gloves to do this part of the job. Lift the head off. It's okay if pieces of it stick to the clay. They'll burn away during firing, leaving their impression.

5. Unbend the paper clips into S shapes. Bend each S into a slight angle, and slip it into the center of the back of each tile, about 1 inch below the top edge. This will be the hook from which you'll be able to hang the tiles. If you don't want to hang the tiles, skip this step.

6. Place the tiles on the board in a cool, dry place for about a week. When the tiles are dry and no longer feel cold when held up to your cheek, carefully place them in a pit kiln (see page 30) to fire them.

7. After the tiles are fired, rinse them off to remove any remaining ash. Color across the surface of each tile with chalk or white conte crayon. Be careful to keep the chalk out of the seed head impression. If crumbs of chalk fall into the impression, blow them out.

8. When you have enough white on the surface of the tile that the black or gray impression shows clearly, gently brush the entire surface with acrylic matte medium to keep the chalk from smearing.

A pit kiln is one of the most ancient methods of firing pottery. Centuries before people built kilns out of brick or metal, they fired their pots and bowls in pits like this one.

What You'll Need

A shovel

Dry sawdust and/or dry cow manure

A rack from an oven or a barbecue grill

Old newspapers

Matches

A large metal garbage can lid

5 bricks or brick-sized stones

An adult helper

What to Do

1. Dig a circular pit with sloping sides about 2 feet in diameter and about 18 inches deep in the middle. Dig the pit in open ground, away from bushes and trees and tall grasses.

2. Place a 3-inch-deep layer of sawdust and/or manure in the bottom. Put the oven rack on top of this layer.

3. Arrange the pieces to be fired on the rack so that there is at least 1 inch of space around all sides of each piece. Fill any bowls or other containers with sawdust. If there are too many pieces to fit on the rack, it's okay to cover the pieces on the rack with about 4 inches of sawdust and to make a second layer of pieces over the first one. If you do this, put the heavier pieces on the bottom.

4. Cover the pieces with at least 12 inches of sawdust and/or manure. Fill in the sloping sides of the pit with more manure or sawdust. Level off the top of the pit.

5. Pleat and twist sheets of newspaper into long thin lighters. Lay these in a single layer on top of the filled pit. Place a brick on each of the four sides of the pit, close enough together to support the edges of the garbage can lid.

6. Get an adult to help you with this step! Light the newspaper twists. After they are burning well, balance the garbage can lid on top of the bricks, and weight it down with the remaining brick or stone. The flames should die down shortly. You can tell the sawdust is burning if smoke continues to come from under the lid.

7. Let the pit kiln burn overnight or at least for 6 or 7 hours. It isn't necessary to stay with the pit the entire time it is burning. Once the flames have died down, it's safe to leave. For safety, post a warning sign nearby telling people not to disturb or touch the kiln.

8. When the firing is completed, remove the lid with a stick (it may still be hot), and carefully dig through the ashes to find your primitive fired pottery.

In Search of the Lost...
Landfill?

When you think of an archaeologist, you might think of a person who searches ancient pyramids for mummies of the long-ago rich and famous, or who discovers lost gold in deep-in-the-jungle Incan tombs.

Well, many archaeologists *do* lead exciting lives. But often the "treasure" they find isn't exactly in a spectacular place.

An archaeologist's job is to study the way people lived in the past by examining the objects they left behind. Works of art from a great king's burial site may tell part of the story—but they don't always say much about the day-to-day lives of ordinary citizens.

So to an archaeologist, everyday things—a broken cookpot, a bit of burned food, a worn tool—are really important finds. Each is a piece in the who-were-these-people-and-how-did-they-live puzzle.

Now, think about it: Where would an archaeologist exploring your town 500 years from now find the greatest number of everyday objects from the greatest number of people, all in one place? That's right: the local landfill, or dump. To a scientist studying the past, there's no richer "treasure trove" than the place where the people threw away their trash.

In many early societies, that place was the community or family fire pit, where meals were cooked and the leftovers tossed in to burn. Bits of charred bone and food such as grains and nuts tell an archaeologist what kind

Adventures in "Garbology"

To see how archaeologists learn about the past by studying old trash, conduct your own "garbology" experiment. Pretend that the wastebasket in your room is a long-lost dumping ground or fire pit. Starting at the top, list the items it contains. Is the trash in the middle the same as the stuff at the bottom or the top? How much time passed since the oldest things (at the bottom) were thrown away? Do any of the objects tell you what the person who used them was doing? Are there layers of different kinds of "artifacts" of diet the people ate, what sorts of animals and plants lived in the area, and much more.

Finding the site of the village pit kiln reveals another kind of "trash pile," where potters tossed pottery that came out of the kiln broken or imperfect. Sometimes a pit kiln site is littered with hundreds of clay-vessel pieces. Each is a valuable clue about the humans who lived there.

Some archaeologists study more recent times. In many cities today, urban archaeologists dig through turn-of-the-century garbage dumps, unearthing such things as old toys, tools, newspapers, medicine bottles, and even clothing. Their discoveries help explain city life 100 years ago.

And where do you suppose archaeologists studying early farm life dig for trash treasure? Country families didn't have landfills. They threw things away in a completely different sort of place: the outhouse!

for different parts of the week or times of day? If you compared the trash in your room with the trash in your best friend's room, what would be different? What would be the same?

An archaeologist learns to "read" objects almost as though they were words in a book. The more you read, the better you understand the whole story.

Radioactive Dating

"Radioactive dating" sounds like something teenage space aliens do. But actually, it's how curious earth creatures called scientists figure out the ages of fossils, rocks, and artifacts.

All living things have radioactive atoms inside them called *carbon 14*. The atoms aren't dangerous. They come from the carbon dioxide in air. Plants "breathe" it in, animals eat plants, and people eat plants and animals. So we're all a little bit radioactive.

When something dies, it stops taking in carbon 14. And the radioactivity already in the plant or animal starts to gradually decay, or fade away.

Scientists know exactly how fast (well, actually, how slow) carbon 14 loses its "buzz." After 5,730 years, half the radioactivity is gone. And after about 50,000 years, there's none left at all.

By measuring how much radioactive carbon 14 is still in a piece of wood, shell, bone, or fossil, scientists can tell how long ago it was a part of something alive. And if it has no radioactivity, they know that it's more than 50,000 years old.

Of course, rocks don't eat or breathe so they don't contain carbon 14. But when most rocks are formed they do pick up other kinds of radioactive atoms, which also decay at a certain speed.

HAPPY 1,300,000,000TH BIRTHDAY, ROC!

SPECIMEN NO. ....: 50% ARGON 50% POTASSIUM

When lava from a volcano hardens, for instance, it almost always contains brand-new radioactive potassium 40. It takes 1.3 billion (1,300,000,000) years for a rock to lose half its radioactive potassium 40 atoms. Those atoms don't really go anywhere, though. As they decay, they turn into a kind of un-radioactive atoms called argon 40.

So, to figure the age of volcanic rock, scientists compare the number of potassium 40 atoms with the number of argon 40 atoms. A rock that's half and half is 1.3 billion years old. (Can you guess how old a rock is if it has twice as many potassium 40 atoms as argon 40 atoms?)

Fantastic
Fossils

Fossils are the remains of animals and plants that lived long ago—*really* long ago. Dinosaur fossils are at least 65 million years old. The earliest fossils known, tiny bacteria from ancient sea deposits in southern Africa, are 3-1/2 *billion* years old.

Most things that die are eaten up by animals or bacteria before they get a chance to *be* fossils. But sometimes mud or sand quickly covers the dead animal or plant. The soft parts decay, but hard parts, such as bones, teeth, shell, or wood, last longer. Over the ages, minerals from soil or water seep into the buried parts, making them tougher. Eventually they're hard as rock. They become *petrified*, like the stone logs in Arizona's Petrified Forest National Park, or the dinosaur bones and eggs at Utah's Dinosaur National Monument.

Other times, even the hard parts dissolve. The entire plant or animal disappears, but it leaves an impression of itself in the rock—a *mold*, much like the seed tiles you can make on page 28. Fossilized footprints are another type of mold. Sometimes minerals fill in the mold and make a *cast* fossil. (If you poured plaster of Paris into a footprint in your backyard, you would be making a cast.)

By comparing fossils from different places around the world and from different layers of rock, scientists can "read" about Earth's development.

Often, the stories fossils tell are surprising. Fossilized sea life, for instance, has been found in rock at the top of Mt. Everest. So we know that what is now the world's highest mountain was once the bottom of an ocean. And where do you suppose scientists have found the remains of a lush tropical forest? Buried under miles of ice and snow—at the South Pole!

Actually, if it weren't for fossils, you'd have a hard time believing most of the crazy stories you hear about life on Earth millions of years ago.

A reptile four stories high and as heavy as 15 elephants? A fish as long as an 18-wheeler, with the head of a huge snapping turtle?

Yeah, right!

Ferns as tall as oak trees? Twenty-foot-long centipedes? Dragonflies with 2-1/2-foot wingspans?

Get outta here!

But scientists know that all these things—and a whole lot more about Earth's incredible history—are absolutely, undeniably true. They're facts written in stone: fossils.

Spider Web

The orb-web spider makes a sturdy web that covers a large area yet uses little material and energy. The spider makes a spiral path beginning at the center. After you make this model web, you'll never look at a spider web in the same way again!

What You'll Need

A piece of cloth 12 by
12 inches*

An iron and ironing board

A 10-inch wooden embroidery
hoop**

A needle

Silver or white embroidery
thread

Scissors

*Look for cloth that's made for counted cross-stitch or embroidery, in a color that you like. Or you can use any medium-weight to heavy-weight cloth that's not textured and not silky.

**Get this at a craft or sewing store.

What to Do

1. Iron the cloth if it is creased or wrinkled.

2. Loosen the adjusting screw on the embroidery hoop, and separate the two parts of the hoop. Lay the cloth, centered, over the inner (smaller) hoop; then place the outer hoop over the cloth and the inner hoop,

and push down equally all around. The cloth will be stretched tightly by the hoops. Tighten the screw when the outer hoop is in place to lock the whole arrangement. You can then gently pull out any wrinkles or loose spots in the cloth.

3. Thread the needle with several feet of thread. Pull the two ends of thread together and knot them. You will be using a double strand of thread. When you run out of thread, just tie a knot on the back of the cloth, and start a new piece of thread just as you did this first piece.

4. An orb-web spider begins its web by laying down a bridge line between two upright supports, such as branches or fence posts.

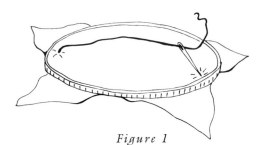

Figure 1

You'll do this by poking your needle from the back to the front of the cloth at any spot as close to the edge as you can. Bring the needle and thread across the circle of cloth, and put the needle in as close to the hoop as you can on the opposite side of the circle. See Figure 1. Now stick the needle back out toward the front, very close to the spot where you just came from. Swing all the way across the circle, and put the needle back in very close to where the bridge line began. You should now have a double thickness of bridge line, and the needle should be on the back side of the cloth.

5. The orb-web spider next attaches a strand near the middle of the bridge line and reels out silk to drop to another anchoring point, pulling on the bridge line so that a Y shape is formed.

You'll do this by bringing the needle and thread (on the back side of the cloth) to a spot on the edge midway between the two anchoring points, poking the needle through, and looping it up and around the bridge line. Just poke the tip of the needle through, so that if it isn't in the right spot, you can easily pull it out and try again until it comes out exactly where you want it. Now bring the needle across the front side of the cloth, and stick it back in at a spot on the edge

midway between the other two anchoring points. Pull a little on the thread (and be sure that it loops around the bridge line) so that it pulls the bridge line into a slight Y shape. On the back of the cloth, travel up to the center again, poke the needle through, and retrace the bottom leg of the Y so that it has double thickness like the other bridge lines. See Figure 2.

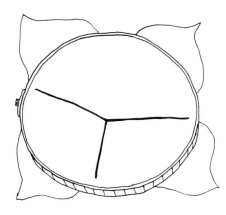

Figure 2

6. The next thing the orb-web spider does is to lay out a framework of spokes that move outward from the center of the web.

To copy her, move the needle over about 1 inch from the bridge line, staying at the outside edge of the circle, and poke the needle through to the front side. Then bring the needle across the front of the cloth to the center, and poke it through to the back. Take the needle to the edge of the cloth, about 1 inch from the spoke you just made, and poke it through to the back. Repeat these huge stitches until you've made spokes all the way around the web. Each time you come back to the center, bring the needle out as close to the same place as you can. See Figure 3.

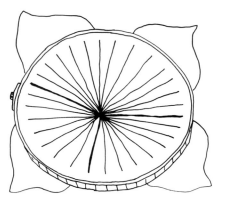

Figure 3

7. After all the spokes are in place, the orb-web spider builds a spiral outward from the center. As the spiral turns, the distance that the web moves out along the spokes remains the same with each turn.

In your case, make a spiral by poking the needle through so that it comes out the center on the front of the cloth. Move out about 1/4 inch and poke the needle through *right next to* any spoke. On the back side, feel around with the needle until you find the spot just on the *other* side of the spoke from where you went in, and poke the needle back to the front. See Figure 4.

Figure 4

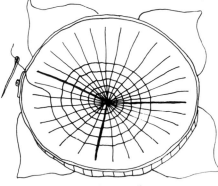

Figure 5

8. Continue moving in a spiral. Study Figure 5 carefully. As you move, try to keep the spaces that you move along the spokes the same. The spaces between the spokes will, of course, grow larger as you move out from the center.

9. When your web is the size you want it to be, add a few more anchoring threads. The outer edges of spider webs are never perfectly smooth.

10. If you've enjoyed making an orb-web spider web, study some other spiders as they build webs. Draw their webs, and make some notes about what they do first and how they proceed to build their webs. Then embroider their webs the same way you did the orb-web. You can make a collection of spider web models.

Amazing Spiders and Incredible
(Edible?) Webs

Did you know that some spiders live *underwater*, in little air-filled spider-web balloons? Or that some capture their meals by hurling gluey spitballs at passing bugs? Others lasso their prey with spider-silk rope!

Spiders are among the most amazing creatures on earth. Scientists think there are somewhere between 30,000 and 50,000 different kinds in the world. Even the most common types, such as garden spiders and other members of the family known as orb weavers, are anything but ordinary.

Orb weavers spin the kind of web you think of when you picture a spider web: a round or triangular net of silky threads. Next time you see one, take a closer look.

See those wispy, almost invisible silk strands spiraling round and round the web? Each is less than 1/100 of an inch thick, yet stronger, by weight, than steel. If you look at one of the strands under a microscope,

you'll see little drops of sticky liquid strung along it, like beads. That's what bugs get stuck in. Inside each tiny bead is more spider silk, coiled up like a spring. When a trapped insect struggles, the coils unwind and the strand stretches, so the bug can't break free. Sticky spider silk can stretch more than four times its length without breaking!

Have you ever wondered why spiders don't get caught in their own webs? It's because not all the threads are sticky. In an orb web, the strands that extend outward from the center like spokes on a wheel are dry. When a spider runs to a trapped insect, it steps only on the dry strands and not the gluey ones.

Most orb webs contain about 60 feet of silk and take a spider about half an hour to build. If a part of the web gets damaged, the spider eats up all the wrecked pieces and patches the holes with new silk. Some orb weavers gobble up their old webs and build new ones every day!

Collection Box

Sooner or later, every collector faces the problem of what to do with all the rocks, shells, bones, feathers, seed pods, and other specimens he or she has gathered. If you find yourself with a bag full of unsorted treasures, this nifty collection box might be just the thing you need.

What You'll Need

9 large matchboxes*

Acrylic paints

A paint brush

A razor knife

9 brass paper fasteners

A couple of handfuls of cotton

9 small, blank, self-adhesive labels (or some big ones to cut up)

A small corrugated cardboard box as close as possible to the size of the 9 matchboxes stacked in three rows of three and pushed close together. (Be sure the box is larger than you need it to be, not smaller; you can trim a larger box to fit.)

Cellophane tape

Scissors

Self-adhesive shelf paper

White craft glue

*Or more, or fewer, depending on the size of your collection. These directions are for a 9-drawer unit.

What to Do

1. First make the drawers. Empty all of the matches into a large container, such as an old coffee can. You won't need the matches for this project, so give them to a grown-up.

Each matchbox has an outer covering and an inner drawer. Paint one of the ends of each box's drawer with acrylic paint. This drawer end is the only part of the matchbox that will show in the finished collection box.

2. After the paint is dry, carefully cut a tiny slit (1/8 inch long) in the very center of each painted drawer front. Make the cut in a vertical (up and down) direction. Insert a paper fastener through each tiny slit, and bend back the two legs of the fastener to make a drawer pull for each drawer. See Figure 1.

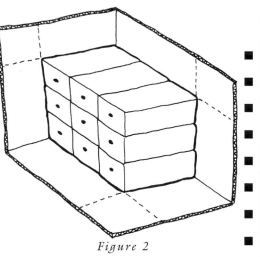

Figure 2

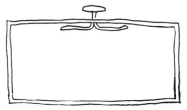

Figure 1

3. Fill each drawer with a layer of cotton, and replace each drawer in its outer covering.

4. Now make the case to hold all the drawers. Stack the drawers inside a corner of the corrugated cardboard box. Make three stacks of three drawers each. Use a pencil to mark on the cardboard box where the top, sides, and front of the triple stack fall. See Figure 2.

5. Use the razor knife to trim away extra cardboard from the box, cutting along the marks you have made. If you are cutting down a larger box, you will have to add one or maybe two sides. Use scraps of cardboard or pieces of another cardboard box and cellophane tape to fasten on the needed extra pieces. When you finish, you should have an outer case without a front that holds the nine drawers snugly in place.

6. Remove the drawers from the corrugated case. Cover the outside of the outer case with self-adhesive paper.

7. Replace the drawers in the outer case. You should be able to pull open each drawer easily without moving the others. If neighboring drawers move or pull out when you open a drawer, you will need to glue the sides, top, and bottom of each matchbox to its neighbors. To do this, first remove all the matchboxes from the outer case. Begin by putting white glue on the top and one side of one of the matchboxes. Push a second matchbox against the gluey side, and place a third matchbox onto the gluey top. Continue to glue the rest of the matchboxes together until you have glued all nine in their triple stack. Now return the stack to the cardboard outer case. You might also need to glue the triple stack to the inside of the case in the same way. Let the glue dry thoroughly, and again test the drawers. They should open and close easily without moving their neighbors.

8. Place your collection in the drawers, and write the identification of each piece on the labels. Some collectors also like to add a card inside each drawer that tells where and when the specimen was found.

Rock On, Earth Planet!

Geology is the study of the Earth's crust. Millions of years ago (almost 5,000 millions!), our planet's surface was a boiling, bubbling, molten mass. You wouldn't have wanted to be here. But gradually things cooled down. Gases in the air formed water. The hot surface turned solid, creating a crust. Finally, about 400 million years ago, living creatures emerged and began making a home for themselves on land.

Down below, our planet is still a fiery soup. Sometimes, where the Earth's crust is thinnest and weakest, the molten stuff breaks through: Lava erupts from a volcano. In other places where the crust is cracked, the surface might suddenly shift: An Earthquake happens. This sort of thing has been going on for a long time. Our planet's crust seems stable, but actually it's constantly moving, shifting, cracking, and pushing. Over the ages, the surface has gone through a lot of changes. Great masses of land have jammed together, shoving up the chunks of rock we call mountains. Whole continents have broken apart, creating smaller continents.

One way to get to know the Earth's crust better is to study its rocks. By collecting them and figuring out how they were made, you can get a glimpse of our planet's birth and childhood.

Igneous rock. The word *igneous* means "fire." This is rock that was once molten liquid deep inside our planet. Some kinds of igneous rock came flying or gushing up out of the Earth in volcanic eruptions. Others cooled and hardened before they made it all the way to the surface, but were exposed later by wind and rain. Granite is a common igneous rock. Basalt and obsidian are igneous rocks, too.

Sedimentary rock. This is rock that started out as silt, sand, or smashed-up seashells floating in water. Eventually the tiny bits settled to the bottom, where they built up in thick layers. All that weight squeezed the grains together. Meanwhile, minerals in the water seeped into the spaces between the particles, bonding them into solid rock. Limestone and chalk are sedimentary rocks made from pulverized seashells. Shale was once mud or clay. And sandstone is a sedimentary rock made from—well, you know that!

Metamorphic rock. It's not easy being a rock way down under the surface. All that heat and pressure and crunching around can really change you. That's what metamorphic rock is: igneous or sedimentary rock that's been pressure-cooked into a whole different, tougher breed of rock. Marble is the rugged, metamorphic version of an old softie, limestone. Slate is the hard-rock relative of its flaky cousin, shale.

A Rock and *a Hard Place*

What's the difference between a rock and a mineral? Minerals are to rocks what flour and water are to bread: the basic ingredients. A particular kind of rock always contains the same minerals, but not always in the same amounts. Granite, for instance, is an igneous rock containing grains of the minerals feldspar, quartz, and mica. One piece of granite might contain a lot of feldspar and just a little mica and quartz, while another might have less feldspar and more mica or quartz. But still, both pieces are granite.

Minerals, on the other hand, always have a specific chemical identity. For example, the mineral quartz always contains the same chemical elements in the same amounts—one part silicon to two parts oxygen. Some pieces of quartz are clear, some are rose-colored, some are smoky-looking. But all are chemically the same.

Hypsometer

How in the world can you measure something as tall as a large tree or a skyscraper? A hypsometer (hip-SOM-uh-ter) is the answer. This clever instrument uses triangles to measure the height of very tall things.

What You'll Need

A cardboard tube about 2 feet long

Acrylic paints

A paint brush

A piece of corrugated cardboard about 6 by 6 inches

A pencil

A razor knife

An awl or a large nail

Colored plastic tape

Scissors

A needle

2 feet of black or other dark-colored thread

A yardstick

A piece of heavy poster board

or cardboard 18 inches long by 1-1/2 inches wide

2 heavy rubber bands

A piece of wood, such as molding, about 2 feet long by 1/4 inch thick by 3/4 inch wide

A fine-tipped black permanent marker

3 feet of heavy thread or kite string

A fishing weight or a washer or other small weight that can be tied to the thread

A stapler

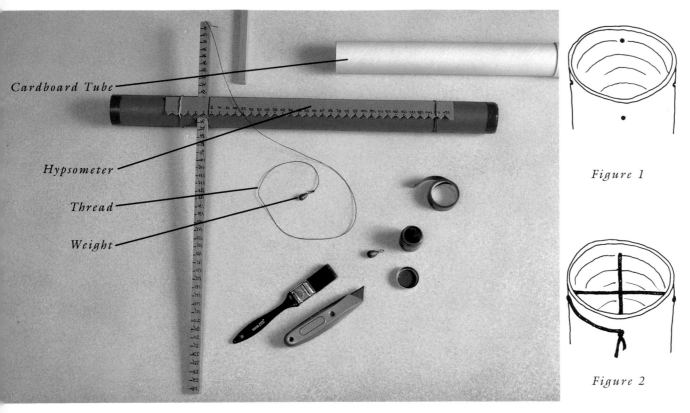

Cardboard Tube

Hypsometer

Thread

Weight

Figure 1

Figure 2

What to Do

1. First paint the tube if you want your hypsometer to be fancy and decorated. If you don't want to decorate it, skip this step.

2. After the paint is completely dry, stand the end of the tube on the piece of cardboard and trace around the circular end with a pencil. Use the razor knife to cut out this circle.

3. Punch a small hole in the exact center of this circle with the awl or large nail. Then tape the circle to one end of the tube with plastic tape.

4. Use the awl or nail to poke four small holes in the other end of the tube. The holes should be about 1/4 inch down from the opening and spaced equally around the opening. See Figure 1.

5. Thread the needle with dark-colored thread. Poke it

through one of the holes and pull the thread from the outside, through the hole, across the opening of the tube, and into the hole on the opposite side. (Hold the tail of the thread with your finger to keep it from sliding through the holes.) Now, without cutting the thread, bring the needle to one of the other two holes. Poke the needle in and pull the thread from the outside, through the hole, across the opening of the tube, and through the hole on the opposite side of the opening. You should now have a cross made of thread in the opening. Tie the ends of the thread together and trim the remaining thread. See Figure 2.

6. Wrap plastic tape around the outside of the opening in this end of the tube to hide the holes and thread ends.

7. Now make the height measure. Lay the piece of poster-board alongside the yardstick and mark off every 1/2 inch, using the permanent marker. Make each mark 1/2 inch long. Do NOT number the marks yet. See Figure 3.

8. Use scissors or the razor knife to cut a sawtooth edge. Begin each cut between two marks, cut at a slant to the bottom of one mark, then cut at a slant up to the spot halfway between the next mark and the mark you are on. See Figure 4.

9. Use the rubber bands to fasten the height measure to the tube. See Figure 5.

10. Now make the distance measure. Lay the piece of wood next to the yardstick, and make the same marks as you did on the poster board height measure. Number these marks, beginning with 0 and going by 5s until you run out of marks.

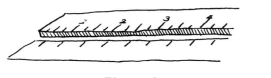

Figure 3

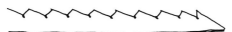

Figure 4

Figure 5

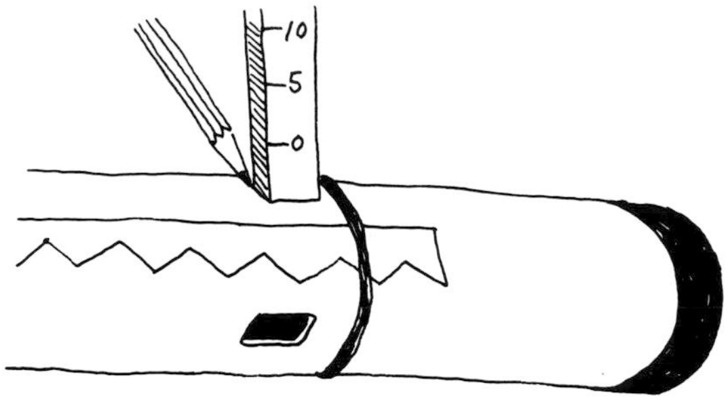

Figure 6

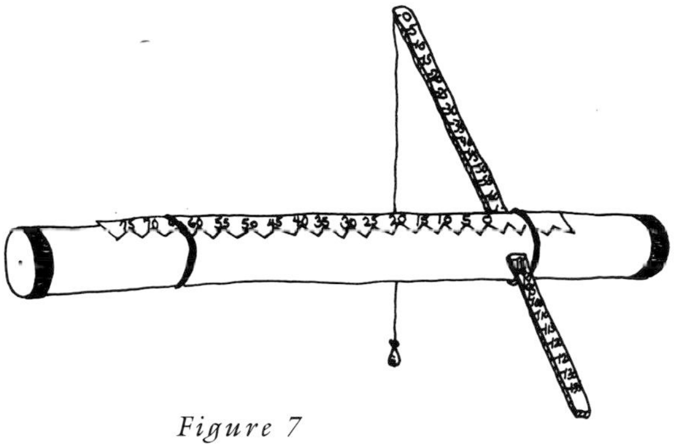

Figure 7

11. Hold the wooden distance measure with one of its ends against the tube, about 6 inches down from the end with the crossed threads and right beside the height measure. See Figure 6. Trace around the end of the wooden piece. Use the razor knife to cut this shape out of the side of the tube. Now trace the end of the wooden piece on the cardboard tube on the other side of the sawtooth measure. Figure 6 also shows you where this place is. Use the razor knife to cut out this shape, too.

12. Slide the wooden distance measure through the two shapes you have just cut out of the tube. The wooden measure should be firmly held in place, yet it should easily slide up and down through the cutout shapes.

13. Tie one end of the heavy thread or kite string to the fishing weight (or whatever you are

using as a weight). Staple the other end of the string to the 0 end of the wooden distance measure.

14. Now you are ready to number the height measure. Start numbering at the first mark after the place where the distance measure is inserted into the tube. Going from right to left, begin with 0 and number by 5s until you run out of marks. There will be a few notches and marks on the other side of the wooden measure. Just leave those without numbers. See Figure 7.

15. To use the hypsometer, measure the distance from where you are standing to whatever it is you want to measure. You could use a long tape measure or a yardstick. (Note: You must be on level ground or at least on the same level as the object you are measuring.)
Slide the wooden distance measure so that the number of

feet you are from the object is at the opening where the wooden measure goes into the tube (away from the sawtooth edge). Hold the hypsometer so that you can look through the pinhole while the weighted string swings freely on the same side of the hypsometer as the sawtooth edge. Turn the hypsometer until the string hangs free.

Look through the pinhole so that the top of the object to be measured is at the cross point of the crossed threads. Now gently turn the tube so that the freely hanging weighted string catches on the sawtooth edge. Carefully lower the hypsometer, making sure that the string does not move from the tooth in which it is caught. Add your height to the number on the height measure where the string was caught. The sum is the height of the object. Note: If you are measuring the object in feet, be sure to add your height in feet.

43

THE AIR

around us—we breathe it every

minute of every day. Yet air is

important to us in other ways, too.

If you build some wind chimes from

clay pots, you can discover how

sound travels through the

air....Make a xylophone, and listen

to the different notes that come from

tubes that hold different amounts of

air....Build a nephoscope to help you

track the clouds as they move across

the sky....Make a hot air balloon

and a rocket jet kite—why should

rocket scientists have all the

fun?...Build a barometer, and tell

your friends what the weather will

be like tomorrow....Or make a new-

tech hovercraft, a helicopter, and a

wind speed meter—and learn even

more about the air around us.

AIR

Clay Pot Wind Chimes

These chimes have a nice, musical sound on a breezy spring or summer day. Play around with different sizes of pots to get different tones.

What You'll Need

Several clay flowerpots of different sizes

Scissors

Rope

Monofilament fishing line

Broken pieces of pottery or seashells

A paint brush

Acrylic paints

What to Do

1. Wash and dry the pots, if they have been used.

2. Cut a piece of rope about 3 feet long, and tie two or three knots right on top of one another at one end. The knots should make a big lump.

3. Thread the unknotted end of the rope through the hole in the bottom of the pot, from the inside out. See Figure 1. The knot should stop the rope from coming out of the pot.

4. Cut a piece of monofilament

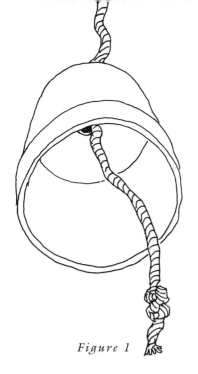

Figure 1

about 8 inches long. Tie one end of it to a piece of broken pottery or a shell.

5. Reach into the pot and pull the knotted rope out so that you can tie the other end of the monofilament to it. See Figure 2. Adjust the length so that the bottom edge of the clapper hangs out of the pot by about 1 inch.

6. Make as many bells as you want, perhaps using different sizes of pots and different materials for the clappers.

Figure 2

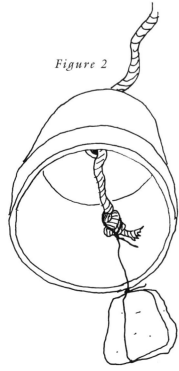

7. Paint designs on your bells with acrylic paint.

8. When they are dry, hang the bells outside where the wind can move them.

What's That Sound?

Throw a rock into the middle of a pond, and circles of waves ripple outward. Blow your nose in the middle of a room, and circles of a different sort of waves ripple outward. You can't see them, but you hear them: H-O-N-K.

When you blow your nose you make it vibrate, and when it vibrates, your schnozzola makes the surrounding air vibrate, too. Waves of air molecules, some thick and some thin, go rushing outward in a special you-blowing-your-nose pattern. When the waves reach your ear, they make your eardrum vibrate in exactly the same pattern. Your inner ear changes those vibrations to electrical messages and passes them along to your brain. H-O-N-K.

All sounds happen like that. When something vibrates, it wiggles back and forth in its own special way. As the vibrating thing pushes forward into the air, the air molecules in front are squashed together and the molecules behind are thinned out. When it pushes back again, it squishes together the molecules behind it and thins out the ones in front. Every time the object vibrates, it pushes out more thick and thin groups of air molecules: sound waves. Different patterns of sound waves produce different sounds.

An object that vibrates slowly (your nose, for instance) makes a low sound. Things that vibrate fast have a high sound. We call how high or low a sound is its *pitch*, and the number of times something vibrates per second its *frequency*. Which would have a higher pitch: something that vibrates 100 times a second, or something that vibrates 300 times a second?

You can change an object's pitch by changing its thickness. Have you ever noticed that some of the strings on a guitar are thicker than others? The thickest string vibrates the slowest and has the lowest pitch. The thinnest string vibrates faster, and makes a high note.

You can also change an object's pitch by changing its length. Shorter things vibrate faster and produce a higher sound. If you're playing a guitar, you can make a string sound a higher note by pressing down on the string and shortening its length. (Check out the two photos above.) Look at the xylophone on page 48. When you bonk one of the tubes, the metal and the air inside the tube vibrate and send out sound waves. Which tubes make the highest notes: the long ones or the short ones?

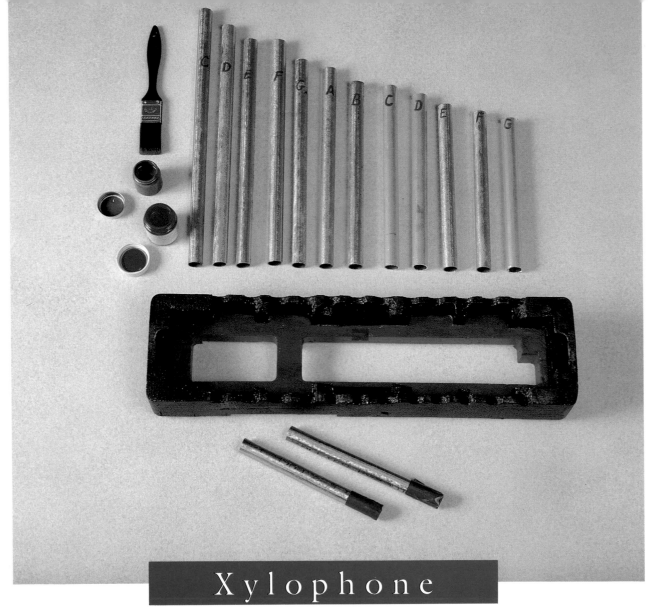

Xylophone

A xylophone with clear, ringing tones can cost a lot of money. You can make this one for very little cost, and you'll enjoy playing your favorite songs, as well as inventing new tunes.

What You'll Need

12 feet of 5/8-inch aluminum or steel pipe*

A ruler

A hacksaw

A metal file

A plastic foam packing form at least 16 inches long by 5 inches wide with an open center, or 2 pieces of foam packing form 16 inches long by 1 inch wide. Whichever of these that you use should be between 1 and 2 inches high.

A razor knife

Acrylic paint

A thin paint brush

A wide paint brush

12 inches of colored plastic tape

Scissors

*Metal pipe is available from a hardware store.

What to Do

1. Saw the pipe into the following lengths: 14-1/4 inches, 13-1/4 inches, 12-1/2 inches, 12-1/4 inches, 11-1/4 inches, 10-3/4 inches, 10 inches, 9-3/4 inches, 9-1/4 inches, 8-3/4 inches, 8-1/2 inches, 8 inches, 7-1/2 inches, and 7-1/2 inches.

2. Use the file to smooth the sawn ends.

3. Arrange the pipes in order from long to short. Keep the two 7-1/2- inch pieces out of this arrangement. Using the thin paint brush, paint

48

each of these letters on the end of a pipe, starting with the longest pipe: C, D, E, F, G, A, B, C, D, E, F, and G.

4. Use the knife to cut two shallow resting places for each pipe on the foam forms. See Figure 1.

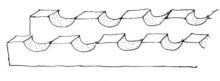

Figure 1

5. Paint the foam base your favorite colors, using acrylic paints and a paint brush.

6. Arrange the pipes in their resting places, beginning on the left with the longest pipe, C.

7. Wrap 6 inches of tape around one end of each 7-1/2-inch pipe. Hold the short pipes by the taped ends when you play the xylophone.

Totally
Tubular

Every minute of every day, you're surrounded by background noise: a hodgepodge of sound waves, with all sorts of frequencies and pitches. Usually, you hear all the sounds at once, jumbled together. But here's a way to partially sort them out.

Save the cardboard tubes from a roll of wrapping paper, a roll of paper towels, and a roll of toilet tissue. Or better yet, cut several long tubes into a variety of lengths—say, 6, 12, 18, 24, 30, and 36 inches. Now put an end of each tube to your ear, one at a time, listen into the end of it, and compare the sounds.

Why do you hear only low, soft sounds in the long tubes, and only higher, louder sounds in the shorter tubes?

All things have their own *natural frequency*, or range of frequencies, at which they vibrate. One way to make that happen is to hit or (in the case of a rubber band or guitar string) pluck the object. But that's not the only way. If sound waves come along that have the same frequency as an object's natural frequency, the waves will make the object vibrate, too. Scientists call this *resonance*. Maybe you've noticed it when you've been listening to a stereo and a certain note made something in the room vibrate and buzz.

That's what's happening in the tubes. The "object" that's vibrating is the column of air inside each tube. Because each tube is a different length, the air column inside "hears," or resonates with, only the sounds that match its frequency range. So it picks up the background sounds that it "likes," and ignores the rest.

49

Sound Viewer

With this easy-to-make device, you can create a light show that will let you *see* sound.

What You'll Need

A small, empty can, such as a tomato paste can or a baking powder can

A can opener

Acrylic paint

A paint brush

A large balloon

A heavy rubber band

Scissors

Tiny pieces of broken mirror, or small pieces of very shiny silver foil paper

Super glue

What to Do

1. Remove both ends of the can and wash it out.

2. Paint the outside of the can with acrylic paint to decorate it.

3. After the paint is dry, make a rubber membrane by cutting a section out of the balloon and stretching it across one of the open ends of the can. Hold the rubber membrane in place with the rubber band. Adjust the rubber band so that it is tight, and pull out any wrinkles from the membrane so that it is smooth and tight across the opening.

4. Use a tiny bit of glue to glue a small piece of mirror or shiny silver foil to a spot near an edge of the membrane. The mirror or foil should not touch the edge of the can.

5. When the glue is dry, go to a sunny window, and hold the sound viewer so that it reflects a spot of light onto a wall while you hold the open end of the can up to your mouth. You may have to move around some to find the right position.

6. Now talk and hum into the can while pressing it up against your face around your mouth. Notice what happens to the light when you sing very high notes, when you talk in a deep voice, when you sing a musical scale.

7. Try making a second sound viewer. This time glue several pieces of mirror or foil to the rubber membrane in a design. Watch what happens when you sing or talk into this viewer.

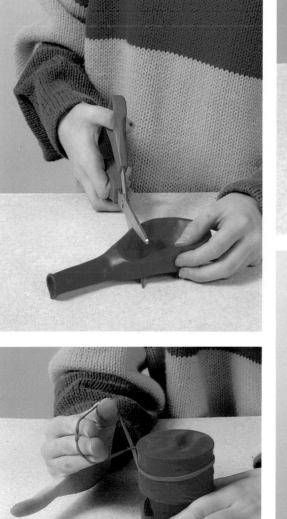

Nephoscope

A nephoscope is an instrument that makes it easy to see which direction clouds are traveling in—which can be hard to do with the naked eye. You can make this nephoscope in just a few minutes.

What You'll Need

A piece of glass or plexiglass about 5 by 10 inches

A piece of black paper the same size as the glass or plexiglass

A piece of plywood, Masonite, or heavy cardboard about 12 by 18 inches

Plastic tape, 1 inch wide

Sandpaper

A magnetic compass

Acrylic paints

A paint brush

Stencils for letters (optional)

What to Do

1. Lay the piece of black paper in the center of the board, and place the glass or plexiglass on top of it, so that the paper is completely covered by the glass.

2. Carefully tape the glass and the paper to the board. Cover all of the edges of the glass with tape.

3. Smooth the edges of the board with sandpaper. Brush

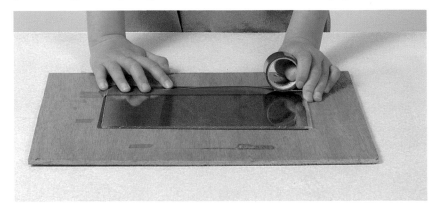

off all the dust from sanding. (If you are using cardboard, you can skip this step.)

4. Use acrylic paints to paint the letters N, S, E, W, NW, NE, SW, and SE on the board in the same positions in which they appear on a compass. Stencils will make it easier to paint the letters, but you can also do them freehand. If you want to, paint a background around the letters.

5. To use the nephoscope, go outside and hold the board so that N points to north when the board is held flat. Look in the glass, and you will see a reflection of the sky. Watch the clouds float across the mirror surface; you will be able to see the direction from which the clouds come.

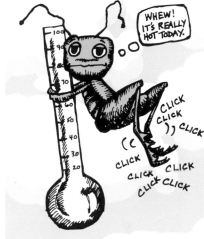

Jiminey Cricket, *It's Hot!*

Have you ever listened to the pleasant chirping of crickets on a summer's night? If you're wearing a watch, the crickets will not only sing to you but also tell you the temperature!

How? Just count the number of chirps a cricket makes in one minute. Then divide that number by four, and add 40. More often than not, the figure you get will be within two or three degrees of a thermometer's air-temperature reading.

Like other insects, crickets are cold-blooded creatures. In other words, their body temperature is always at the same temperature as their surroundings. Crickets are more active in warm weather. They chirp by rubbing the bases of their back legs together. And the warmer the temperature, the faster they rub!

Hot Air Balloon

This is a tricky project but well worth the fine-tuning it takes to get your balloon aloft. The trick is to be sure the air outside the balloon is much cooler than the air you put into the balloon.

What You'll Need

12 pieces of colored tissue paper, each 20 by 30 inches

White craft glue

A stapler

A marker

A ruler or yardstick

Sharp scissors

Old newspapers

A hair dryer

What to Do

1. Run a thin bead of glue along the short edge of a piece of tissue paper, 1/4 inch from the edge. Overlap a second piece of paper over the glue so that the two pieces are joined and make one long piece of tissue paper 20 inches wide and about 5 feet long. See Figure 1.

Figure 1

2. Repeat Step 1 five more times until you have six long sheets of paper.

3. Fold each long sheet of paper in half lengthwise, and stack the six sheets exactly on top of one another. Keep all folded edges on the same side.

4. Be sure all edges are even; then staple the stack together along the unfolded edges and at the top and bottom. See Figure 2. Put the staples about 10 inches apart, and be sure not to put any staples on the folded edge. The staples will make it easier to cut the pieces of paper all at one time.

5. Use the marker and ruler to mark the top sheet of tissue paper like Figure 3. (Just put the dots. No need to write the measurements. The measurements just tell you how far to put the dots from the folded edge and from each other.)

6. Join the dots with a curving line. See Figure 4. You should have a gentle curve. Carefully cut through the whole stapled stack of paper at once along the curved line. You will have cut off the stapled pieces and will be left with a stack of folded papers.

7. Put the first folded piece of paper on top of some sheets of old newspaper. Put a piece of newspaper between the two layers of tissue, to keep the glue from seeping through. Run a thin bead of glue along the curved edge of the top sheet.

8. Place the second piece of folded tissue paper on top of the first, gluing the curved edges together. See Figure 5.

9. Slip newspaper between the two layers of tissue paper on piece number two.

10. Repeat Steps 7, 8, and 9 for the rest of the six sheets of

tissue paper. You should end up with a stack of tissue paper sheets folded on one edge and glued together like an accordion on the other, curved edge. Let the glue dry completely before going on. See Figure 6.

11. When the glue is dry, carefully take out all of the newspaper. Some of it will be stuck to the tissue paper, and you will have to peel it away in the stuck spots.

12. Open out the bottom piece of tissue.

13. Put a thin bead of glue all along the curvy edge, just as you did in Step 7.

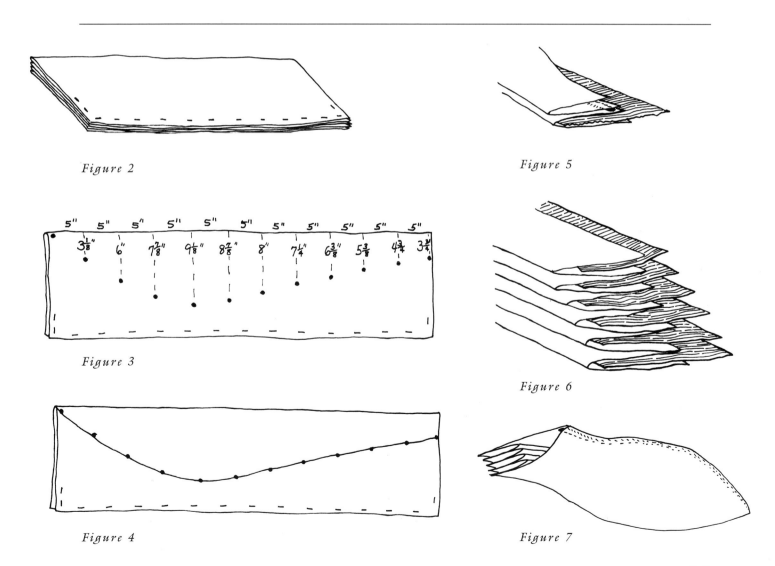

Figure 2

Figure 3

Figure 4

Figure 5

Figure 6

Figure 7

14. Unfold the top piece of tissue paper and press its curvy edge all along the bead of glue. See Figure 7. The balloon pieces are now all joined.

15. Wait for the glue to dry completely before inflating the balloon. While you are waiting for the glue to dry, you can glue tissue paper streamers to the bottom edge for decoration if you like. Cut thin strips about 24 inches long, and glue one to each of the six sections of the balloon.

16. Ask a friend to help you hold the balloon upright while you carefully place a hair dryer just inside the open bottom of the balloon. (If you put the dryer too far into the balloon, the dryer will overheat and turn itself off.) When the balloon is inflated and all puffed out, it should rise to the ceiling.

17. Fly your balloon outside only on cool or cold days when there is no breeze. Use an extension cord to plug in the hair dryer. If you are flying your balloon outside, you might tie a kite string to it as a tether to keep it from getting away from you. Be sure to fly it in an area without trees.

When you fly your balloon inside, try to find a cool room with a high ceiling so you can watch the balloon lift as if by magic. When the air inside it cools and the balloon comes down, simply inflate it again with the hair dryer. *Happy flying!*

Rocket Jet Kite

A jet kite works on the same principle as an old-fashioned balloon rocket, but it's a showier version. The challenge is keeping the envelope materials light enough for the balloon to jet-propel it. You and your friends can spend a rainy afternoon having jet kite races!

What You'll Need

A supply of long, skinny balloons

A cloth tape measure

Sheets of colored tissue paper

Scissors

White craft glue or a glue stick

A plastic drinking straw for each kite

Cellophane tape

A reel of monofilament fishing line or kite string

What to Do

1. Blow up a balloon. Ask someone to hold it closed while you measure it around its fattest width. Write down the measurement. Now measure its length, and write down that measurement, too. Let the air out of the balloon for now.

2. Put two sheets of tissue paper on top of each other. On the top piece, draw a rectangle that is as long as your blown-up balloon and 2 inches wider than *half* of your balloon's width. Find the mid-point of one of the short sides of the rectangle, and draw lines from that point to points 1/3 of the way down each of the long sides. See Figure 1.

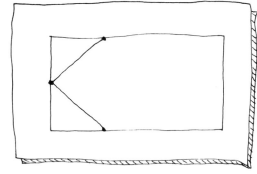

Figure 1

3. Cut out the two pieces of tissue paper at the same time.

4. Run a thin bead of glue along both long sides and the pointy end of one of the tissue paper shapes. Lay the other shape on top of the first shape, and press the gluey edges together. If you want to decorate the kite, use a small dot of glue to glue on sequins or pieces of other colors of tissue paper. Be careful not to let the kite get too heavy.

5. After the glue has dried, cut fringe along the unglued edge of the tissue paper envelope.

6. Cut the plastic drinking straw to a 6-inch length. Tape it to one side of the tissue paper envelope with 2 small pieces of cellophane tape. See Figure 2.

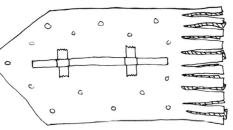

Figure 2

7. Thread one end of the monofilament through the straw. Tie that end to the back of a chair. Pull the monofilament tight and out about 20 feet. Cut it, and tie this end to the back of another chair.

8. Blow up the balloon. While holding the neck tight, slip the balloon inside the tissue paper envelope. Move the jet kite down to one end of the monofilament line. Be sure the kite's pointy end is facing the long part of the string.

9. Count "One! Two! Three! Go!" and let your jet kite fly. If you want to have races, each kite will need its own line.

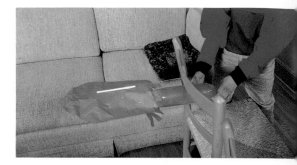

What Makes a Rocket *Rocket?*

"...three...two...one...ignition...liftoff!" With a roar of fiery engines and a huge cloud of smoke and vapor, the space shuttle rises from Earth's grasp and heads for outer space.

"...three...two...one...*brrrazzel errrt*...plop!" With a burst of whoopee-cushion noise, a toy balloon careens crazily through the air and lands with a thump on the sofa.

Believe it or not, both "rockets" use the same sort of "engine" to make them fly. Scientists call it the action-and-reaction principle. It says that for every action, there is always an equal but opposite reaction.

When you blow up a balloon and hold the end shut, all the air inside pushes outward evenly against the balloon's walls. The balloon doesn't go anywhere because the push on each side of the balloon is equal to the push on the opposite side. All the forces are equal. Nothing is moving.

When you let go of the end, though, everything changes. The push on the front of the balloon isn't balanced by air pushing at the back. Instead, there's no push at the back. So the balloon leaps forward. The action of the air rushing out in one direction causes an equal reaction in the other direction.

The same thing happens inside a rocket. Rocket engines produce hot gases inside a chamber that has an open end. The hot gases push against the chamber's walls and rush out the open end with tremendous force. That action causes the spectacular reaction we've all witnessed: *whoosh!* Another rocket soars into space at thousands of miles per hour!

Centipede Kite

A centipede kite is a wondrous thing to see. Follow carefully the directions for building the kite, but let your imagination run wild when you decorate its face and arms.

What You'll Need

A piece of poster board cut into 11 strips 28 inches long and 1 inch wide

Scissors

A stapler

A pack of colored tissue paper

A light-colored pencil or a piece of chalk

Glue (rubber cement, glue stick, or other glue that won't wrinkle paper)

A black marker

Scraps of white typing paper

11 very thin bamboo garden stakes about 26 inches long

A hole puncher or an awl

Kite string

What to Do

1. Staple each strip of poster board into a ring.

2. Lay one ring down on a piece of tissue paper, and carefully trace around the circle with chalk or a light-colored pencil.

3. Draw another circle 1 inch outside of the first circle you

drew. Cut out the second (larger) circle.

4. Make cuts from the edge of the cutout circle to the inner circle about 1-1/2 inches apart. These will be glue tabs.

5. Put a bead of glue all around the outside of the poster board ring.

6. While the glue is still wet, set the ring on the inner circle of the tissue paper circle. Press the glue tabs up all around the ring so that the tissue paper is stretched smoothly all around the ring.

7. Repeat Steps 2 through 6 for each of the 11 rings.

8. Make one of the rings into a face, using markers, white paper scraps, and tissue paper scraps. Add ruffles around the edge, streamers, or whatever looks good to you.

9. With the hole puncher or awl, punch three holes in each ring—one at the top and one at

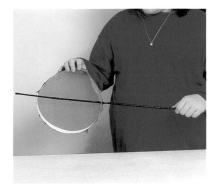

each side. Be sure the side holes are exactly across from each other at the center of the ring.

10. Carefully push a bamboo stake through the side holes of each ring. Center each stake, so that its side arms are of equal length.

11. Glue tissue paper scraps to the ends of the bamboo arms for more decoration.

12. Cut 30 pieces of kite string, each about 8 inches long.

13. To assemble the centipede,

use the arms of a chair or the sides of a big cardboard box to balance all the armed rings. Put the rings in the order you want them to be in the finished kite. Tie three strings between every two rings. See Figure 1.

14. Make a bridle on the face ring. Cut three strings, each a foot long. Tie one to each arm where the arm meets the ring, and tie the third string to the hole in the top of the face ring. Bring the ends of the three strings together in front of the face. Tie the strings together. See Figure 2.

15. You can hang the kite from the bridle and one or two other rings. Or you can tie the bridle strings and one or two other rings to the tops of poles for a parade. Your centipede will move like a wave in the breeze if you hang it near a window. It will make a fine, fierce mascot at the front of a parade.

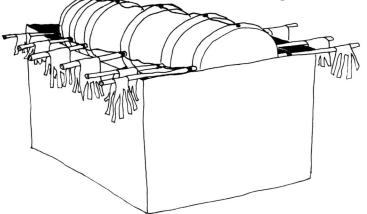

Figure 1

Figure 2

Hidden *Air*

Riddle: You can't see me, but you can see the space that I fill. What am I?

Answer: air that hides in liquid.

You probably know several liquids that have air hiding out in them. How about cola drinks? Hard cider? Root beer? Ginger ale? Ginger beer? Fizzy liquids have carbon dioxide in them. (Carbon dioxide is one of the gases that make up our air.)

How does the air get in there? One way is through a process called *fermentation.* Some drinks, such as ginger beer, are made by mixing tiny, one-celled plants called yeasts with fruit juice or sugary water.

Yeasts are plants with no chlorophyll, so they can't make their own food the way green plants can. Instead, they must get their food from their surroundings. In the case of ginger beer, the yeasts eat sugary lemon juice and water. While eating, the yeasts breathe out carbon dioxide, the same gas that humans breathe out. And since the yeasts are living in a liquid, the carbon dioxide makes a space for itself in the liquid—tiny air bubbles.

As the yeasts eat and breathe, they also multiply, and soon they release many bubbles of carbon dioxide into the liquid. As long as the bottle is kept tightly capped, the air stays in the liquid. But as soon as the bottle is opened, the carbon dioxide begins to escape, causing the tingly feeling that fermented drinks give your tongue.

Barometer

A barometer is a basic weather-forecasting tool. Once you've begun to take note of changes in air pressure, you'll have a good idea of what to expect of the weather over the next day or so.

What You'll Need

A large balloon, 11-inch size or larger

Scissors

A quart-sized (or larger) glass jar with a wide mouth

About 12 inches of strong string or yarn

2 plastic drinking straws

Super glue

Two straight pins, extra long if possible

A shallow cardboard box, about 15 by 10 by 2 inches

Acrylic paints

A paint brush

A permanent black marker

What to Do

1. Cut off the neck of the balloon and stretch the balloon over the neck of the jar. Pull the balloon tight so that there are no bubbles or dimples in the surface. Tie the balloon to the neck of the jar with string. Wrap the string several times around so that it holds the balloon tightly. See Figure 1.

Figure 1

2. Cut a 4-inch length of one of the straws. Slit up one end about 1-1/2 inches. See Figure 2. Bend the slit ends to form a base for the straw. Notch the uncut end of the straw to form a resting place for the other straw. See Figure 3.

Figure 2

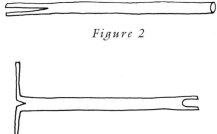

Figure 3

3. Glue the bent base of the straw to the center of the balloon with Super glue. While the glue is drying, trim one end of the other straw to a point. This will be the pointer of the barometer.

4. After the glue is completely dry, place the second straw sideways through the notched end of the upright straw. The pointer end should be on the right. Hold this straw in place with a pin. See Figure 4.

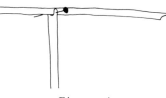

Figure 4

5. Remove any flaps from the box, and decorate it with acrylic paint. When the paint is dry, stand the jar apparatus in front of the box. With the top straw in a level position, stick the second pin through the straw about 1 inch to the right of the first pin. Stick this second pin all the way through the straw so that it sticks out the other side and into the box, loosely holding the straw to the box. You will have to push the jar as close as possible to the box. Even so, the upright straw may slant slightly inward. There should still be about 1 inch of pin between the straw and the box.

6. Place the barometer in or near an open window. Watch what happens to the pointer end of the top straw as the weather changes. Use the marker to record the position of the pointer and the weather at the time the straw was in that position. After a few days you should be able to see some relationship between the position of the straw and the weather. The pressure of the air in the room on the balloon causes the straw to move up and down. What happens when there is high pressure? What happens when the pressure is low?

Wind Facts That'll *Blow You Away*

The highest wind speeds on earth are produced by tornados. Meteorologists believe that some tornados produce winds as high as 400 miles an hour. The scientists don't know for sure, though, because the twisters always wreck their wind-speed instruments.

The strongest side-to-side wind ever recorded blew on April 12, 1934, at a weather station on Mount Washington, New Hampshire, USA. Observers measured a gust blowing 231 miles an hour!

The windiest place in the world is Commonwealth Bay, King George V Coast, in Antarctica. Winds average more than 70 miles an hour most of the year. You definitely wouldn't want to be there during a storm. Winds come howling in at 200 miles an hour!

The human body produces some impressive wind speeds, too. When you breathe normally, air moves in and out at a respectable five miles an hour. When you sniff, air comes gusting in at 20 miles an hour. That's a Force 5 on the Beaufort Scale; enough, according to the Scale's description, to make "small trees sway and small waves develop on lakes and rivers."

And when you sneeze hard: Stand back! That blast of air is moving 100 miles an hour—faster than many hurricanes!

Wind Sock

A wind sock tells you from which direction the wind is coming. This one looks like a school of fish darting and swimming together.

What You'll Need

1/2 yard each of 3 different colors of taffeta or ripstop nylon

Scissors

Old newspapers

Fabric glue*

Scraps of other colors of light-weight material for decoration

6 plastic glue-on eyes**

About 36 inches of 14-gauge galvanized steel wire or other easy-to-bend wire

Wire cutters

Monofilament fishing line or kite string

An awl or a big nail

A cup hook

Pliers

A swivel hook

An old broom handle or a piece of 3/4-inch dowel, about 48 inches long

  *Fabric glue is available in fabric stores.

**Eyes can be bought in craft stores.

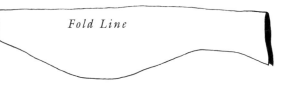

What to Do

1. First make the fish. Begin by folding one of the pieces of taffeta or ripstop in half length-

Fold Line

Figure 1

wise. Cut a fish shape, as shown in Figure 1, being careful not to cut into the fold of the cloth. Your fish's body should be about 30 inches long. Save any

66

scraps of material to use as deco-ration on other fish. Unfold the fish. Put a layer of newspaper under the entire piece of cloth.

2. Cut scales and other shapes out of other colors of cloth. Glue these in place with fabric glue. Also glue on two eyes. See Figure 2.

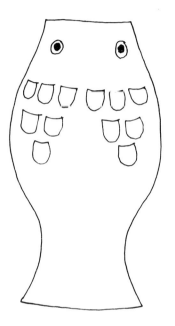

Figure 2

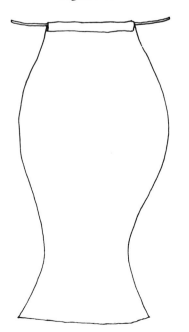

Figure 3

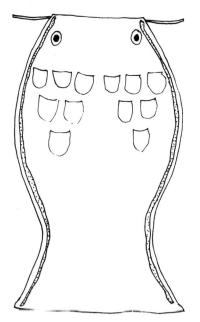

Figure 4

3. When the glue has dried (about 20 minutes), turn the fish over so the decorated side is against the table. Cut a piece of wire 4 inches longer than the width of the mouth end of the fish. Run a bead of glue all along the edge of the mouth end. Lay the wire just inside the line of glue. Fold the fabric over to cover the wire. See Figure 3.

4. When this glue has dried completely, turn the fish back over so the decorated side is up. Run a bead of glue all along the outside edges. See Figure 4.

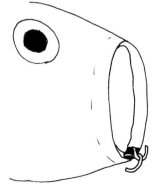

Figure 5

5. Fold the fish over so that the other outside edge is pressed against the bead of glue and the fish has been glued into a sort of fish-shaped tube. Do not glue

the mouth or tail end closed. As you get close to the mouth end, you will have to bend the mouth wire into a hoop. Bend the wires that are sticking out of the mouth end so that they lock together and hold the mouth into a round hoop. See Figure 5.

6. Use the awl or nail to start three holes around the hoop, just inside the wire. Into each hole thread an 18-inch-long piece of monofilament or kite string. Tie these strings to the hoop; then gather the free ends of the strings and tie them together to form a bridle. Make a second knot about an inch down from the first gath-ering knot. See Figure 6.

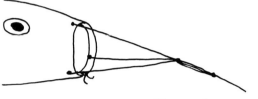

Figure 6

7. Repeat Steps 1 through 6 for the other two fish.

8. Next you'll make the pole. Hook the cup hook through the plain loop end of the swivel hook (the end that doesn't open). Use pliers to squeeze the cup hook closed.

9. Use the awl or nail to start a hole in the flat end of the dowel. Then screw the cup hook (with swivel hook attached) into the end of the dowel. Clip the three fish to the clasping end of the swivel hook. See Figure 7.

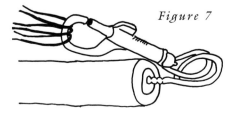

Figure 7

10. Hang the school of fish out of an upstairs window or from a flagpole.

Hovercraft

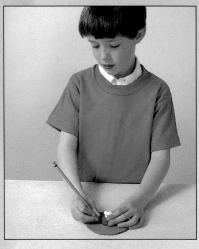

Every day, people travel from the eastern shore of Great Britain across the English Channel to Europe in a strange boat-plane called a hovercraft. The hovercrafts that cross the English Channel have many air jets under them. The pilot fires up an engine that sends so much air out of the jets that the hovercraft actually rests on a thin cushion of air. This air reduces friction and lets the hovercraft scoot freely over the water.

What You'll Need

A piece of corrugated cardboard about 6 by 6 inches

A pencil

Something to use as a pattern for drawing a circle 4 or 5 inches in diameter, such as a large mug or an upside down cereal bowl

A razor knife

Self-adhesive shelf paper

Scissors

A cap from a squirt bottle of liquid detergent—the kind of cap that can be pressed down to close and pulled up to open

White glue (optional)

A 10- or 11-inch round balloon

What to Do

1. Tracing around the pattern, draw a circle about 4 inches in diameter on the cardboard. Cut out this circle with the razor knife.

2. Place the bottle cap in the exact center of the cardboard circle, and trace around it with the pencil.

3. Corrugated cardboard has three layers: a top paper layer, a middle layer of ribbed paper, and a bottom paper layer. In this step you will be cutting through ONLY the top and middle layers of the corrugated cardboard. Use the razor knife to gently slice through the top paper layer just inside the small circle you have traced around the bottle cap. Remove that paper. Now carefully slice through the middle layer of ribbed paper. Be very careful not to cut through the bottom layer of paper. Remove the scraps of the inner layer. You should now be able to see the bottom layer.

4. Use the tip of the razor knife to cut a small square (with 1/4 inch sides) out of the remaining layer of corrugated cardboard inside the small circle.

5. Cover both sides and edges of the cardboard circle with self-adhesive shelf paper. Leave the small cutout circle and the cutout square on the other side uncovered.

6. Wedge the bottle cap down inside the cutout circle. It should fit snugly. If it is loose, put a thin bead of glue around the edges of the small circle, and then wedge the cap in the circle.

7. Press down on the cap to close it. Blow up the balloon. Twist its neck to hold the air in while you fit the opening of the balloon over the valve (top part) of the bottle cap. Be sure that the balloon stands straight up from the cap. Pull on the neck of the balloon to adjust

it. If the balloon leans over, the hovercraft won't work. Release the neck of the balloon. It will release a little air into its neck and then should stand straight up.

8. Grasp the neck of the balloon and the valve and pull up on the valve to open it. Place the hovercraft down on a smooth surface, such as a kitchen counter top or a smooth tile floor, and watch the hovercraft scoot.

9. Try sending the hovercraft down a sliding board on a playground. Compare its speed and performance without the balloon and with the balloon. Try making different sizes of hovercrafts. Try skimming the hovercraft over water. Fill a tub or sink. Let the surface of the water settle until there are no waves or ripples. Place the hovercraft gently on the surface of the water at the same time that you pull up on the valve of the cap. Experiment until your hovercraft stays afloat.

Helicopter

Everyone knows that when you run with a pinwheel the wheel will spin. What happens if you turn a pinwheel on its side and put it on top of a helicopter body? Try dropping this model off an upstairs porch or down a tall stairwell.

What You'll Need

A 6- by 6-inch square of paper

Scissors

Colored markers

A long, straight pin with a round head

A 1/2-inch-long piece of plastic drinking straw

A cork

What to Do

1. Fold the paper once into a triangle. Unfold it, and then fold it into the opposite triangle.

2. Unfold the paper. It should have creases going from corner to corner, forming an X. The center of the X is the center of the square. Make a cut from each corner halfway to the center along each crease. See Figure 1.

Figure 1

3. Use markers to color both sides of the paper and the entire cork.

4. When the paper has dried completely, make the wheel. Pick up any point; stick the pin through the point about 1/4 inch in from the point; skip the next point, but pick up the next and thread it onto the pin just as you did the first point. Continue around the square, threading every other point onto the pin until you have four points threaded onto the pin and four points lying flat. Now stick the point of the pin through the center point of the square. See Figure 2.

Figure 2

5. Slip the piece of drinking straw onto the sharp end of the pin while holding all the points on the pin; then push the end of the pin into the side of the cork about 1/4 inch from one end. Push the pin in firmly, but not all the way in. The straw should be able to move up and down slightly, and the wheel should feel springy.

6. Throw the helicopter up and watch what happens as it drops. The longer the drop, the better, so look around for good launching places such as stairwells, upstairs porches, and balconies.

Riding on *Air*

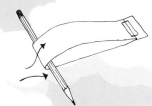

Have you ever been flying comfortably along in an airplane, enjoying the view above the clouds, when suddenly a small, sensible-sounding voice inside you pipes up: "Hey, how can this heavy thing be up here in the air? How come we don't just drop to the ground like a rock?" So much for a carefree trip!

Next time that happens, close your eyes, take a deep breath, and repeat the magic word: Bernoulli. Bernoulli. Bernoulli. (Pronounced Bur-NOO-lee.)

No, Bernoulli isn't an Italian magician. Actually, he was a Swiss scientist (his first name was Daniel) more than 250 years ago. And he figured out something important: Liquids and gases (air, for instance) have less pressure when they're moving. The faster they move, the less pressure they exert.

So what? Take a look. Cut two strips of paper 8 or so inches long and about 1-1/2 inches wide. Hold a strip by one end in each hand, so they hang down side by side in front of you, about 2 to 3 inches apart, with their edges facing you. Now blow hard between the strips, about 2 inches up from the free ends. The strips move *toward each other*—because the moving air between them has less pressure than the still air on either side. The side air pushes harder and shoves the strips inward.

OK, now on to airplanes. Take one of the paper strips and fold it in half. Now scoot the top end back about 1/2 inch and tape or glue it to the bottom. The resulting curved-on-top, flat-on-the-bottom shape is called an airfoil. Look familiar? It's the shape of an airplane's wing.

Slip the folded end of your paper wing over a pencil, and blow hard at the fold. The wing rises and stays there until you stop blowing. What's happening?

When you blow at the wing, your breath divides to pass over and under it, just like air passes over and under the wing of a moving plane. And because the wing's upper surface is curved, the air that goes over the top has to travel farther and faster than the air underneath to get to the other edge. Faster air on top means less pressure on top—and better yet, *more* pressure on the bottom. The bottom air pushes harder and forces the wing upward. The force is called *lift*—but if you're on an airplane, you can just call it reassuring.

Helicopter blades also have an airfoil shape. A plane has to rush forward through air in order for its wings to create lift. But a helicopter has to move only its blades. When they move around fast enough to create a pressure difference, up the 'copter goes.

Wind Speed Meter

Use this simple instrument to estimate the speed of the wind.

What You'll Need

A cardboard box about
7 by 7 by 10 inches

A razor knife

Plastic tape about 1 inch wide

Self-adhesive shelf paper

A coat hanger

Wire cutters

A piece of aluminum foil
about 6 by 8 inches

Scissors

Cellophane tape

A fine-point permanent marker

A Beaufort Wind Force Scale
(see page 74)

What to Do

1. Cut off both ends of
the box. Use tape to reinforce
any pieces that get loose when
the box is cut.

2. Cover the inside and outside
of the box with self-adhesive
shelf paper.

3. Cut a straight piece of wire about 8 inches long from the coat hanger.

4. Poke the piece of wire into the side of the box 1/2 inch in from the open end and 1/2 inch below the top. Push the wire straight across the opening

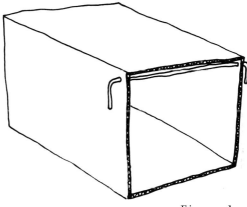

Figure 1

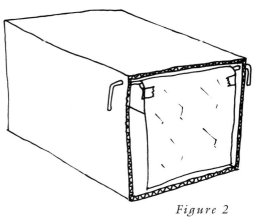

Figure 2

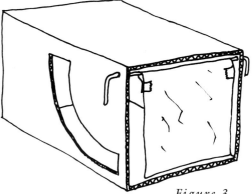

Figure 3

and out the other side. Make sure the second hole is directly opposite the first. Bend the ends of the wire down. See Figure 1.

5. Slide one of the 6-inch edges of the aluminum foil over the wire and make a fold about 1 inch deep all along the folded edge. Tape the fold with cellophane tape so that the foil hangs down like a curtain. Be sure that the curtain can move freely on its rod. See Figure 2.

6. Push on the bottom of the curtain with one finger so that you can see the curved path that the bottom of the curtain follows as it swings inward. Cut a curving slot about 1 inch wide that goes from the bottom of the side of the box to the top, following the path of the bottom of the curtain. See Figure 3.

7. Finish off the edges of the box with plastic tape.

8. To calibrate the meter, place it outside so that the curtain faces the wind. Make a mark where the bottom of the curtain appears. Using the Beaufort Wind Force Scale (see the sidebar on page 74), estimate the wind speed and draw a symbol and/or mark showing the number of estimated miles per hour that the wind is blowing when the curtain is in that position.

It will take several days to completely calibrate the meter; you will have to observe it in many different kinds of wind conditions to fill in the chart. When it is calibrated, you will be able to place it in the wind and estimate the wind speed by reading the position of the bottom of the aluminum foil curtain.

Amazing Easy-To-Use *Wind Force Scale*

To measure wind speeds exactly, weather scientists use an instrument called an anemometer (an-uh-MOM-ih-ter). But you can get a pretty good idea of how fast the wind is blowing just by looking around you.

In 1805, Rear Admiral Sir Francis Beaufort (pronounced BO-fert) came up with a numbering system to describe how hard a wind was blowing by its effect on a Royal Navy ship. For instance, he classified a Force 2 wind as "that in which a well-conditioned man-of-war, with all sail set, and clean full, would go in smooth water from one to two knots." A Force 12 wind was "that which no canvas could withstand."

Today, the Beaufort Wind Force Scale—shown on page 74—also includes descriptions of how wind moves things on land. People all over the world use it to estimate wind speeds.

Force Number	Wind Description	Wind Effects On Land	Miles Per Hour	Kilometers Per Hour
0	Calm	Smoke rises vertically.	Less than 1	Less than 1
1	Light Air	Wind direction is shown by drift of smoke.	1-3	1-5
2	Slight Breeze	The wind is felt on face. Leaves and twigs rustle. Wind vanes move.	4-7	6-11
3	Gentle Breeze	Leaves and twigs are in constant motion. Light flags extend.	8-12	12-19
4	Moderate Breeze	Dust and loose paper blow about. Small branches sway.	13-18	20-28
5	Fresh Breeze	Small trees sway. Small waves develop on lakes and rivers.	19-24	29-38
6	Strong Breeze	Large branches sway. Umbrellas are hard to use.	25-31	39-49
7	Moderate Gale	Whole trees sway. It's difficult to walk against the wind.	32-38	50-61
8	Fresh Gale	Twigs break off trees. Walking becomes very difficult.	39-46	62-74
9	Strong Gale	Slight damage to buildings. Shingles may fly off roofs.	47-54	75-88
10	Whole Gale	Considerable damage to houses and other buildings. Whole trees are uprooted.	55-63	89-102
11	Storm	Widespread damage. (Winds this strong are very rare.)	64-73	103-117
12	Hurricane	Violent destruction.	More than 74	More than 117

Thunder Stick

Also called "rain sticks," thunder sticks are musical instruments that were first made in Africa. They were originally made of bamboo. This version is made out of different materials but has a sound very similar to that of the original instruments.

What You'll Need

5 feet of PVC (plastic) pipe with a 2-inch inside diameter (2" schedule 40)*

36 inches of 1/4-inch dowel

A saw

A brace and bit or a hand drill with a 1/4-inch bit

Sandpaper

6 or 8 pieces of corrugated cardboard, each about 2 by 6 inches

2 large corks, 2 inches in diameter at their smaller ends

Colored plastic tape

1/2 cup uncooked rice

Acrylic paints

Erasers designed to be put over the ends of pencils (optional)

Fat pencils with erasers (optional)

*You can get PVC pipe at a hardware store.

What to Do

1. PVC pipe is usually sold in 10-foot lengths. Ask the sales person to cut the pipe into two 5-foot lengths.

2. Drill a 1/4-inch hole through both sides of the pipe about 8 inches down from one end. Drill another pair of holes 2 inches and a quarter turn farther down the pipe. Drill two more pairs of holes the same distances apart. See Figure 1.

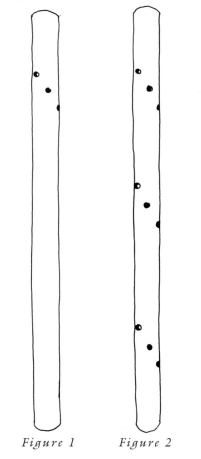

Figure 1   *Figure 2*

3. At the other end of the pipe, drill the same pairs of holes, the same distances apart, as you did in the first end.

4. Drill a third series of pairs of holes in the middle section of the pipe. See Figure 2.

5. Put a dowel through the first pair of holes that you drilled. See Figure 3. It should fit snugly. Saw it off where it comes out of the sides of the pipe. See Figure 4. Sand the pipe and the ends of the dowel smooth. Fill

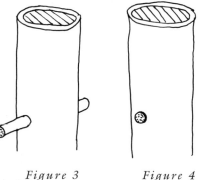

Figure 3   *Figure 4*

all the pairs of holes with dowels in the same way.

6. Fold one of the pieces of cardboard into an accordion fold. See Figure 5. Stuff it

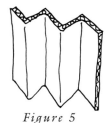

Figure 5

down one end of the pipe until it stops at the first dowel. Fold another piece of cardboard the same way, and stuff it on top of the first piece of cardboard. Put in as many pieces of cardboard as will fit.

7. Plug a cork into the end of the pipe, and tape the cork securely to the end so that it can't come out.

8. Pour the rice into the open end of the pipe. Fold cardboard and stuff it into this end of the pipe just as you did on the other end. Put in all the cardboard that will fit snugly. Cork and tape this end.

9. Decorate the thunder stick with colored plastic tape and acrylic paints. The design on the thunder stick shown here was made by spreading paint in the bottom of an old pie tin and then pressing the flat end of a pencil eraser into it to print the solid circles. The open circles were printed with the open end of an eraser designed to be put over the end of a pencil.

10. To use the thunder stick, practice tilting it slowly back and forth until you can keep a steady pattering sound going. Close your eyes, and listen to the gentle rain.

The Shocking Truth . . .
About Lightning and Thunder

Lightning is a giant spark in the sky, created by static electricity—the same kind of electricity that makes your hair crackle when you brush it, or that gives you a small shock when you walk across a carpet and then touch a metal object (ouch!). If the room was dark, you might've even seen a spark. How'd that happen?

When your feet rubbed on the carpet, you picked up some extra *electrons*—negatively charged pieces of atoms—from the rug. You charged yourself. Then, when your finger came close to metal, you discharged yourself—the wayward electrons flowed through your body and leaped across the air between you and the object with enough force to blow the air atoms apart and give off light and sound.

The same kind of thing happens, only on a *much* more powerful scale, when water droplets and ice particles move and swirl around inside a thundercloud. Scientists don't all agree on exactly how those bumping, blowing, freezing, and thawing particles supercharge a cloud with static electricity. But there's no arguing about the result: Sooner or later, there's a lot more electricity in the cloud than it can hold, and—c-r-r-a-a-a-c-k—like the spark that jumped from your hand, lightning streaks from the cloud to another cloud, or to the ground, a building, a tree, or (gulp) sometimes even a person. (The best place to be in a thunderstorm is *out* of the storm, indoors and away from windows.)

Lightning releases a huge amount of energy. A big flash can cause the temperature of the air around it to rise as high as 54,000° F (30,000° C). That's more than five times hotter than the surface of the sun! The extreme heat makes the air expand suddenly and spread out in powerful waves, like the air around an exploding bomb. Ka-boom! Thunder.

You usually see lightning before you hear its thunder, but actually they happen together. It's just that light travels much faster than sound. To tell how close a thunderstorm is, count the seconds between the lightning and the thunder. It takes sound five seconds to travel a mile. So if you count 10 seconds between the flash and the boom, the storm is two miles away.

Our planet's atmosphere is a shockingly electric place. Scientists say there are about 45,000 thunderstorms in the world every day, or about 16 million a year. In fact, at any given moment there are 1,800 thunderstorms flashing and crashing in our sky. Lightning strikes the Earth 100 times a second!

WATER—

*the stuff of oceans and lakes, rain
and snow, cold drinks and hot baths.
Make a wave in a bottle, and hold
the ocean in your hands....Create a
waterspout, and some litmus paper
to help you tell acids from
bases....Decorate some colorful marbled paper, and build your own
backyard mini-pond....Make an
underwater viewer, so you can watch
underwater life in streams and
ponds, and a skimmer net to help
you catch it....Build a model grist
mill, and you'll discover how we
humans have turned grain into flour
for centuries....Mix up some gluep
and oobleck—wonderful water-
based materials that are fun to touch
and even more fun to play
with....Then make boats from clay
or from wood—and watch them
skim over the surface of the water.*

WATER

Wave in a Bottle

Peek into this model while you tip it back and forth to see firsthand how waves are formed and break up. You control this tiny ocean. You can create a calm, sunny day, or whip up a storm at sea!

What You'll Need

A glass bottle*

Vegetable oil

Water

Food coloring

A cork to fit the bottle
(or the bottle's own cap)

*A flat bottle, such as an old whiskey bottle, works best, but any clear bottle will do.

What to Do

1. Wash out the bottle, and remove the label by soaking the bottle in warm water.

2. Fill 1/2 of the bottle with water. Add a few drops of food coloring (stop when you like the color). No need to stir it.

3. Fill the remaining space in the bottle with vegetable oil.

4. Cork the bottle. If you have a screw-on cap for the bottle, put the cap on the bottle tightly.

5. Turn the bottle on its side, and let it settle for a few minutes. The water should sink to the bottom, and you should be able to see clearly the line between the colored water and the oil. Now begin to tip the bottle back and forth. Experiment to see what kind of waves you can make. If the oil starts to get bubbly, let the bottle rest for a few minutes.

How Waves Work

Ah, the beach. Soaring seagulls. Sun and sand. Waves rolling to the shore and crashing, one after another after another after another, in endless watery rhythm.

As you watch, you might think that the water in the waves is rushing toward you. But it's not. When a wave passes through the water, the water simply rises up, and then comes down again in pretty much the same place. Only the wave itself travels forward. You can see the same effect at home. Ask a friend to hold one end of a rope while you hold the other. Now, shake the rope up and down. Waves travel through the rope. But the rope stays put in your hands.

In open water, waves can travel for thousands of miles. But when a wave approaches shore and passes through shallower water, it slows down. The lower part of the wave starts to drag along the bottom. Meanwhile, the top part keeps going. So the wave curls over itself—and "breaks."

Most waves are formed by the wind blowing across the water's surface. The harder and longer the wind blows, the higher the wave. Earthquakes and other violent underwater movements of the Earth sometimes cause huge waves called tsunamis (soo-NAH-meez). A tsunami can speed through the ocean at nearly 500 miles an hour. Just before it strikes land, a tsunami sucks water up into itself and away from the coast, sometimes for several miles. The wave can rise as high as a 20-story building. Then the wall of water slams into the shore, causing great destruction.

Scientists have set up an early warning system in parts of the world, such as the Pacific, where tsunamis are most likely to happen. If they think a giant wave is coming, the scientists broadcast an alert so people can go to a safer place.

Waterspout

You can buy a special gadget to connect two plastic bottles, but for just a few pennies you can make this waterspout-maker. Warning: Once you make one waterspout, you'll probably have to make another one for your friends, or you'll never get a chance to play with yours!

What You'll Need

Two 2-liter plastic drink bottles

A flat washer with a 3/8-inch hole

Pipe thread seal tape*

Soft, flexible, plastic tape or electrician's tape

Scissors

*You can buy this at a hardware store or discount mart.

What to Do

1. Fill one of the bottles about 2/3 full of water.

2. Place the washer on the opening of this bottle. Wrap pipe thread tape around the edge of the washer and the edge of the opening of the bottle until the washer is completely sealed to the bottle opening. See Figure 1. Do not cover the opening in the washer. A good seal should take four or five turns of the tape. (The tape isn't sticky like most tapes; you must press it against the surface you want it to hold onto.)

3. Balance the empty bottle on top of the sealed washer and bottle. Hold the bottle in position, and put pipe thread tape around the place where the two bottle openings come together. See Figure 2. Wrap the tape several times so that there is no crack left.

4. Wrap plastic tape or black electrician's tape around the two bottle necks, making a strong joint. You'll need to wrap it several times. Completely cover the pipe thread tape and all the neck space of the two bottles. See Figure 3.

5. Turn the bottles over so that the filled bottle is on top. Check the joining for leaks. The water should just barely drip from bottle to bottle.

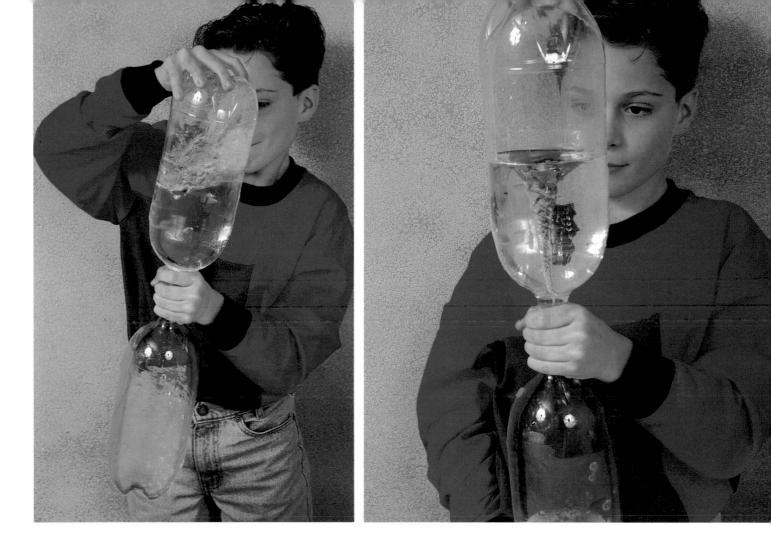

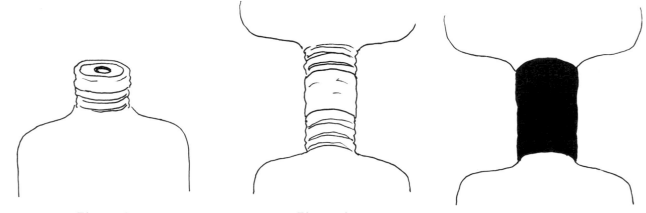

Figure 1   *Figure 2*   *Figure 3*

6. When you are sure the bottles do not leak, hold the filled bottle in one of your hands, and hold the joined bottle necks in your other hand. Holding the bottles horizontally, roll them in a circular motion a few turns; then quickly hold the bottles upright, with the filled bottle on top. If the waterspout does not appear, give the bottles a few more turns. Try turning them in the opposite direction. Within a few tries, you should see a waterspout, a tiny tornado in the water, form. Watch how it draws the water down into itself as the water rushes from one bottle to the other.

Whirlpools and
Rubber Duckies

You're enjoying a nice, relaxing bath in the world's biggest tub. You lean back and close your eyes. Aahhhh, this is livin'.

Yikes! All of a sudden somebody pulls the plug! Instantly you're swept toward the drain into a swirling current. As you spin crazily round and round, you lean over and look down  into the whirlpool's middle. Haalllp! There's nothing but a hole! You're being sucked into empty space! You can't get away! You...

Whoa. Enough of this nightmare. Things like that just don't happen—unless you're a rubber duckie or some other bath toy. Right?

Well, not exactly. There actually *are* places in oceans, lakes, and rivers where rotating currents called *whirlpools* give boats and people trouble. Usually, the currents are formed when fast-moving water runs into a curved bank, or when incoming and outgoing tides move through a narrow passage at the same time. Small ships can get stuck and damaged in a whirlpool, but the water doesn't actually suck them into a hole.

In a bathtub, the spiral of water running down the drain is called a *vortex*. A tornado is a kind of vortex, too. If you make the waterspout project on page 82, you can watch a vortex in action and figure out what's happening. Here's how.

Without rotating or spinning the bottles, turn them over quickly so that the filled one is on top. Glug. Glug. Water drips slowly into the empty bottle, one glug at a time, and then stops completely. Why doesn't the water all run out at once? Because its "skin," or surface tension, holds the liquid back at the small hole where the two bottles meet. Besides, the empty bottle isn't really empty.

It's full of air. The water has to push some of that air out of the way in order to get in.

So every time water glugs into the bottom bottle, it shoves a bubble of air up into the top bottle. And the water level in the upper bottle goes down. Eventually there's not enough water to push down hard enough to shove air aside. Everything stops. (In fact, if the top bottle isn't almost full to begin with, it may not drip water at all.)

Rolling the bottles before you turn them upright, though, puts a new spin on the situation. The water in the top bottle starts rotating. At the same time, gravity pulls the water down toward the narrow drain hole. What happens? The same thing that happens when rotating ice skaters suddenly pull their arms in—they start spinning very fast. The closer to the neck the water gets, the faster it spins. A funnel-shaped vortex forms, with a hole in the middle. Presto: The hole lets air in from the lower bottle and water out from the upper bottle, all at once. Whoosh.

The same kind of thing can turn a bad thunderstorm into a tornado. All strong storms create powerful updrafts of moist air. When conditions are right, crosswinds put spin on the updrafts—just like when you rolled the bottles to make the water rotate. The result is a whirling column of upward-moving air called a "mesocyclone" (MEZ-o-SIGH-klone). Not all mesocyclones turn into tornados. But sometimes, as a mesocyclone spins upward, it becomes much narrower at the bottom than at the top. *That* speeds up the spin. (Remember the ice skater?) The result is a vortex of winds that can whirl faster than 200 miles an hour. If the vortex touches ground, it's a tornado. If it comes down over water, it's a waterspout.

Now, back to your bathtub. When you first pull the plug, water glugs out and then stops, just like the water in the bottles before you rotate them. But then a whirlpool starts, and the water drains freely.

So what makes the vortex? What puts the spin on the water going down the drain? Why, the planet Earth, of course! We're spinning all the time—at over 600 miles an hour!

Red Cabbage Indicator Paper

This kit will let you test liquids to see if they are acids or bases (see the sidebar on page 87). You'll also be able to compare liquids to known acids or bases to see which ones the liquids are most like.

What You'll Need

A red cabbage

A grater

2 bowls

Water

Scissors

Blotter paper (or any heavy, white, non-shiny paper)

An empty potato chip can with its lid

Colored self-adhesive paper

White typing or drawing paper

Markers or colored pencils

Various liquids to test, including lemon juice, vinegar, baking soda, water, milk, orange juice, tap water

Clear self-adhesive paper

What to Do

1. Grate up the cabbage, and let the gratings sit in a bowl of water for several hours.

2. Meanwhile, cut the blotter paper into strips around 6 inches long by 1/2 inch wide.

3. Cover the potato chip can with colored self-adhesive paper.

4. After several hours, drain the red cabbage water into another bowl. (You can use the grated cabbage to make coleslaw.)

5. Soak the strips of blotter paper in the red cabbage water for a few minutes until they turn bluish purple. Lay the wet strips flat on a counter top or other smooth surface.

6. Test some liquids with the indicator strips. (You can do this while they are either dry or wet.) Using markers or colored pencils and the white typing paper, copy the color that the paper strip turns. Draw a picture or write the name

of the liquid that caused the paper to turn that color.

7. Use your notes to make a chart that shows the different colors that different liquids turn the indicator strips. When you test a liquid of unknown acidity, compare the color of its indicator strip with a known liquid's

strip color. Try testing rain, melted snow, stream water, and soil mixed with water.

8. You can attach the chart to the can using clear self-adhesive paper.

9. Keep the indicator strips in the can, where it is dry and dark.

Acids and Bases *and You*

Acids and bases play important roles in our lives. They are in the foods we eat and the medicines we take. They are used to make virtually every product people use, from soap to glass to dyes for our clothes (as shown in the photo at right). Of all the different chemicals in the world, most are either an acid, a base, or a combination of the two.

Acids are sour-tasting chemicals. Lemon juice and vinegar contain acid. So do green apples, grapefruit, tea, and yogurt.

Not all acids are safe to eat, or even touch. Some of the most important acids are so powerful they can burn holes in skin and clothing. Nitric acid and sulfuric acid are two examples. They're used to produce such things as plastics, dyes, fertilizers, and explosives. When mixed with enough water, however, even "industrial" acids can be harmless. Hydrochloric acid is so powerful it will dissolve metal. But watered-down hydrochloric acid is in your stomach right now. Your body makes it to help digest food.

Bases are bitter-tasting chemicals that often have a slippery feel. Soap is made from a base. Egg whites and ammonia are bases. So is your blood. Oven cleaners and drain uncloggers contain the powerful base known as lye, or sodium hydroxide. It, too, can burn skin.

An important idea to remember is that acids and bases are chemical opposites. When you mix them together in the right amounts, they *neutralize* each other. For instance, if you put a drop of lemon juice (an acid) on your tongue, it will taste sour. But if you add a pinch of baking soda, which is a base, the sour taste will disappear.

Many kinds of vegetables and flowers won't grow well in soil that is too acid. So gardeners neutralize acid soil by mixing in calcium hydroxide, a base commonly known as *lime*.

You can tell if a substance is an acid or a base by testing it with an indicator such as the red cabbage paper described on page 85. An acid, such as lemon juice or vinegar, will turn the paper red. A base (try a tablespoon of baking soda dissolved in a small glass of water) turns it purplish green. Different liquids produce different shades, depending on how concentrated the acid or base is. For starters, try aspirin, flour, and toothpaste (mix each with a little water first).

Here's another experiment: Find an anthill and, using a stick, stir up a small section to alarm the ants (be careful not to get bitten). Now put a piece of indicator paper over the ants and wait a few minutes. Pretty soon tiny pink spots will appear on the paper—from the formic acid that ants spray into the air when they feel threatened!

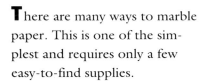

Marbled Paper

There are many ways to marble paper. This is one of the simplest and requires only a few easy-to-find supplies.

What You'll Need

A disposable aluminum cake or lasagna pan

Water

Oil-based enamel paints*

Toothpicks

Several sheets of white and/or colored paper, small enough to lie flat in the aluminum pan

Old newspapers or waxed paper

*You can get small amounts of different colors if you buy paints for model cars and airplanes at craft stores or discount marts.

What to Do

1. Fill the aluminum pan with water.

2. Use a toothpick to stir the oil-based paint; then drip small amounts of paint onto the surface of the water. Use toothpicks to move the paint around; you can swirl it, mix several colors, add drops. Use your imagination, but work rather quickly because the paint will soon form a film on the top of the water. When that happens it will be hard to move the paint around without its clumping and breaking apart.

3. When the design on the surface of the water looks good to you, lay a sheet of paper flat on top of the water. Gently press it to make sure there are no air bubbles. Then slowly lift the paper, starting at one end and rolling it off of the surface of the water. Lay the paper face up to dry on a piece of newspaper or waxed paper.

4. When the paper and paint are completely dry, you can use a warm iron to flatten any pages that are curled or wrinkled. Use your paper for covering small books, making collages, making note cards, or covering small boxes. With experience, you will be able to marble larger and larger sheets. Experiment with different kinds of paper and also with small plastic containers, pencils, and other small objects that you would like to marble.

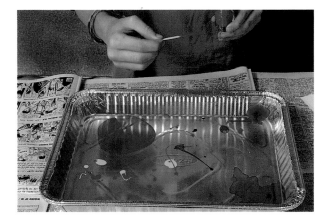

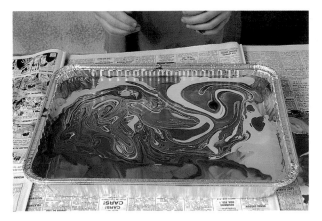

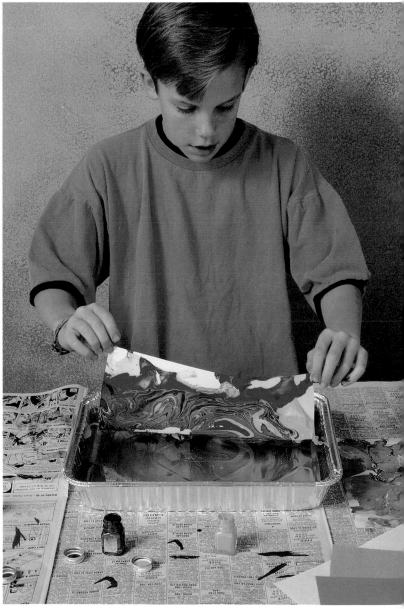

This tiny pond doesn't take up much room, but it makes a nice home for some pond plants—even for a frog and a fish or two.

What You'll Need

A plastic, 30-gallon garbage can (preferably green, brown, or black)

A yardstick or tape measure

Strong scissors

A shovel

Water

Large stones

Goldfish

Floating pond plants

What to Do

1. Select a flat spot for the pond. Either a sunny or shady place will do.

2. Trim off the top few inches of the can, leaving 20 inches of garbage can.

3. Dig a hole as wide and almost as deep as the can. Plan on having 2 inches of the can sticking out of the ground.

4. Place the can down in the hole, and fill in any gaps around it with some of the soil you dug out. Pack it firmly.

5. Fill the pond with water.

6. Place stones around the edge of the pond to hide the rim of the garbage can. Pack soil under and between the stones so that they are firmly held in place.

7. After 24 hours you can add floating pond plants and a gold-fish or two. Ask the pet store for the kind of goldfish that can live in an outdoor pond. Follow directions from the pet store about introducing the fish to the pond. You'll need to feed the fish a few grains of fish food once a day at first, but before long the pond will become home to many small creatures, and the fish will find plenty to eat on their own. If you put in a few elodeia plants (ask at the pet shop), they will add oxygen to the water and make it healthier for your fish.

8. From time to time, scoop out fallen leaves and debris. During dry weather you may need to add water; otherwise the pond will take care of itself. In the winter the top of the pond may freeze, but the fish will swim down to the bottom and partially hibernate. They will stop eating and swim very slowly. When the weather warms up, the pond will thaw and the fish will return to active living. Be sure to keep your pond filled, because if the water is shallower than 18 inches it will freeze completely, and your fish will not be able to live.

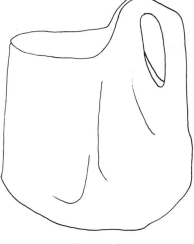

Underwater Viewer

What's happening under-water? This viewer lets you put your eyes closer to the action without getting your face wet.

What You'll Need

A plastic 1/2-gallon milk jug

A razor knife or other sharp knife

Clear plastic wrap

A heavy rubber band

Acrylic paints

A brush

What to Do

1. Carefully cut away the top of the jug, leaving the handle. See Figure 1.

Figure 1

2. Cut away the bottom of the jug.

3. Decorate the outside of the jug with acrylic paints.

4. Cut a piece of plastic wrap 12 x 12 inches. Stretch the plastic wrap over the bottom hole of the jug, and hold it in place with the rubber band. Adjust the plastic so that there are no wrinkles and it is held tightly in place.

5. To use your underwater viewer, hold it by the handle, then press it underwater so that the water comes up the side of the jug but not into it. Peer down through the cut-away top at the stream bottom crea-tures and plants. The water slightly magnifies things, so everything you spy through your viewer will look slightly larger than life.

For centuries water has been used to do work. One of the main uses of water power years ago was to turn wheels in order to grind grain into flour. There aren't very many water-powered grist mills left today, but you can make a working model of one yourself. This model takes time and patience, but when you're finished, you'll be able to see clearly one way that water power can be harnessed to do work.

What You'll Need

Tools

A jigsaw*

Medium-grit sandpaper and a sanding block

2 C-clamps

A pencil

A drill or a brace and bit

A 1/4-inch drill bit

A 1/2-inch drill bit

A 1-inch expansion bit

Wood glue

A ruler

A hammer

A flathead screwdriver

A can opener

A crosscut saw

Materials

2 by 2 feet of 1/4-inch plywood

36 inches of 1/4-inch dowel

11 inches of 1-inch dowel

10 inches of 2- by 4-inch lumber

10 by 6 inches of 1/8-inch plywood

4-1/2 feet of 1- by 4-inch lumber

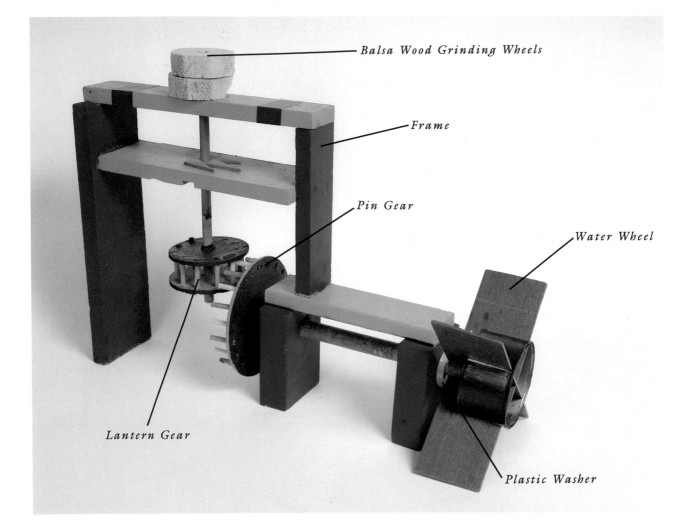

Balsa Wood Grinding Wheels

Frame

Pin Gear

Water Wheel

Lantern Gear

Plastic Washer

13 inches of 3/4-inch doweling

6 inches of 3- by 1-inch balsa wood

A 1-inch or 1-1/2-inch long wood screw with a flat head

A washer to fit the screw

1 plastic washer

A large, empty tuna can, with both ends removed

1 inch of 1-1/2-inch plastic pipe or hose

Several scraps of 1/8-inch plywood

*A power jigsaw is optional but very helpful.

What to Do

1. First make the *lantern gear*. Using the jigsaw, cut out two circles with 3-inch diameters from the 1/4-inch plywood. Sand their edges smooth.

2. Clamp the two circles together onto a workbench. Before you tighten the C-clamp, put a piece of scrap wood that is larger than the circles between the workbench and them. Mark the exact center of the top circle. Then put 11 marks 1 inch apart around the circumference of the circle, 1/4 inch in from the edge. See Figure 1.

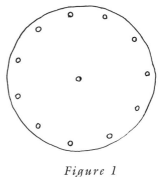

Figure 1

3. With the 1/4-inch bit in the drill or brace, drill the 11 edge holes through both circles at the same time. Then put the 1/2-inch bit in the drill, and drill the center hole through both circles at the same time.

4. Saw the 1/4-inch dowel into 11 1-1/2-inch lengths. Sand the edges.

5. Unclamp the circles. Glue the short dowels into the holes of the bottom circle. Be sure they are standing straight up. Put a dot of glue on the end of each dowel, and carefully fit each hole of the second circle onto the end of each dowel. See Figure 2.

6. Poke the 1/2-inch dowel into the center holes of the two circles so that the dowel sticks 1 inch out of the bottom of the bottom circle. Put aside the lantern gear for now.

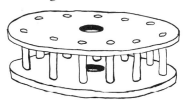

Figure 2

7. Next assemble the *pin gear*. Cut a circle with a 6-inch diameter from the 1/4-inch plywood. Sand it smooth.

8. Mark the exact center of this circle, and also make 19 marks 1 inch apart all around the circumference, 1/4 inch in from the edge.

9. Saw the 1/4-inch dowel into 19 1-1/2-inch pieces. Sand the cut edges.

10. Clamp the circle to the scrap wood and the workbench. With the 1/4-inch drill bit, drill the 19 holes around the edge.

11. Glue the 19 short lengths of dowel into the holes. Be sure the dowels stand straight up. Put aside the pin gear for now.

12. Assemble the *water wheel*. Cut two pieces of 1/8-inch plywood 10 by 3 inches each. Sand them smooth.

13. Mark the center of each of these pieces with a line. Cut halfway along the line. See Figure 3.

Figure 3

14. Fit the two pieces of wood together in an X. If the cut is too narrow for the pieces to fit, make another cut the same length on either side of the first cut to widen it. See Figure 4.

Figure 4

15. Clamp the 1-inch dowel to the workbench with 2 inches of it sticking over the edge. Make two 1-inch-deep cuts at right angles to each other. See Figure 5.

Figure 5

16. Slip the crossed wooden paddles into the crossed cuts on the dowel end. Enlarge the cuts on the dowel if necessary. See Figure 6.

17. Place the crossed paddles on a table with the dowel standing up. Place the tuna can over the dowel, and then center it on the paddles so that the dowel is in the center of the can. Mark the paddles where the tuna can crosses them.

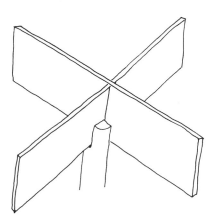

Figure 6

18. Draw a 2-inch line inward on each paddle beginning at the spot where the tuna can mark is.

19. Take the dowel off the paddles and uncross them. Saw each paddle along the 2-inch lines. See Figure 7.

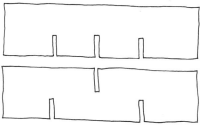

Figure 7

20. Reassemble the paddle wheel. Cross and lock the paddles; slip on the dowel end. Then slide the tuna can into the new cuts. The wheel should be sturdy now. See Figure 8.

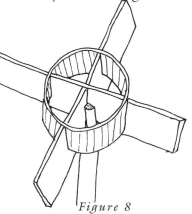

Figure 8

21. Now make the two *grind-ing wheels*. Draw two circles with 3-inch diameters on the wide surface of the balsa wood. Use the jigsaw to cut out the two circles. Since the balsa wood is thick, be careful to saw straight up and down. (It's okay if the circles aren't cut perfectly round.) Sand the circles to smooth them. Then drill a 1-inch hole in the center of one of the circles. Drill a 1/2-inch hole in the center of the other circle. Put these aside for now.

22. Next build the *frame*. Cut the following pieces of lumber:

From 2 x 4 lumber: Cut 2 pieces, each 5 inches long.

From 1 x 4 lumber: Cut one piece 8-3/4 inches long, one piece 8 inches long, one piece 10-3/4 inches long, one piece 12-1/2 inches long, and one piece 13-3/4 inches long.

From now on, we'll refer to all these pieces by the letter names on Figure 9.

23. Using a 1-inch expansion bit, drill a 1-inch hole in A and B, 1 inch down from the top, in the center of each piece. Drill a 1-inch hole in the exact center of E and F.

24. Nail the frame together as shown in Figure 9.

25. Assemble the mill. First, slide the plastic washer onto the dowel of the paddle wheel; then slide the dowel through the holes in A and B so that the washer and wheel rest against the outside of the mill frame.

Slip the 1-inch piece of plastic hose over the 1-inch dowel where it sticks out of the piece A. Now screw the pin gear onto the end of this dowel. Slip the washer onto the screw before putting it into the center of the

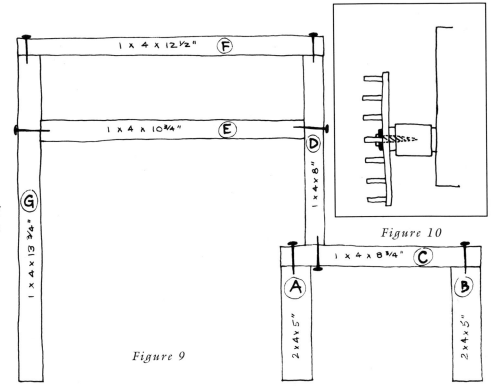

Figure 9

Figure 10

pin gear. See Figure 10.

Glue the balsa wood circle with the 1-inch hole in it onto F, on the top of the frame.

Slide the lantern gear dowel up through the holes in E and F and through the balsa wood circle, as shown in the photo. Adjust the gears so that the short dowels, or gear teeth, of the pin gear connect with the teeth of the lantern gear.

Force the other balsa wood circle over the end of the 1/2-inch dowel. It should fit snugly and hold the lantern gear in place.

If the lantern gear wobbles too much, glue scraps of ply-wood to hold it in position, as shown in Figure 11.

26. Use acrylic paints to paint the mill.

27. To use the mill, place it on a table with the paddle wheel hanging over the edge. Turn the paddle wheel with your hand. Watch how the gears work together to change the direction of motion. Imagine that the two

balsa wood circles are heavy mill stones. Corn and other grains could be ground between the bottom stone and the turning upper stone.

Try the mill in a stream. You'll need to build a dam to force the water into a narrow, fast-moving channel, or mill race. Experiment with the position of the mill and with different ways to speed up and slow down the water in the mill race. Listen to the rhythm of the grinding mill wheels as the water races around the paddle wheel!

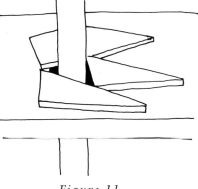

Figure 11

Gearing Up, *Gearing Down*

Gears are wheels with extra bite: teeth that help transfer movement from one part of a machine to another part, so the machine can do its job.

Sometimes gears change the *direction* of movement. Look at an eggbeater. When you turn the crank, your hand moves around in an up-and-down circle. So does the big gear wheel. But the smaller gears on either side change the direction of the movement. The beater blades rotate horizontally, from side to side.

Water wheels use gears to do the same thing. The gears change the wheel's up-and-down motion into the sideways, round-and-round motion needed to turn millstones and grind grain into flour.

Gears also change the *speed* at which machines run, and the amount of *force*, or push, they produce. If two gears fitted together end-to-end are the same size around and have the same number of teeth, they rotate at exactly the same speed and with the same amount of force. But suppose one gear has 40 teeth, and the other is only half as big and has 20 teeth.

One turn of the large wheel will make the small one go around two times, or twice as fast. But each turn

will have only half as much force. On the other hand, if you turn the small gear first, the bigger gear will go around only half as fast, but with twice the force.

By arranging gears of different sizes in different combinations, engineers and inventors can make the moving parts in machines speed up, slow down, or work harder.

Skimmer Net

This net is stronger and more flexible than most nets, because the handle and hoop are all made of one piece of wire. Use it for scooping up water creatures from your pond or from a creek.

What You'll Need

A piece of 14-gauge galvanized steel wire about 3-1/2 feet long

A ruler or tape measure

Wire cutters

Plastic-coated tape

Scissors

A pair of tights or pantyhose (lighter colors are best)

Straight pins

A needle

Heavy cotton thread

What to Do

1. Bend the middle of the wire into a circle about 5 inches across. Twist the wire at the base of the circle to hold the shape.

2. Twist the two long ends of wire together to make a single twisted length of wire. See Figure 1.

3. Bend the long twisted wire in half to form a handle. Then twist the single ends of wire around the section of wire just below the circle. See Figure 2.

4. Tightly wrap tape around the length of wire between the circle and the handle. See Figure 3.

5. Cut a piece of pantyhose as long as the circumference of the circle and about 6 inches wide.

6. Pin the piece of pantyhose net to the circle, turning under about 1/4 inch of cloth as you go. See Figure 4.

7. Pin the side and bottom seams of the net. See Figure 5.

8. Sew the net to the circle where it is pinned. Take out the pins as you sew.

9. Sew the side and bottom seams.

10. When you aren't using your net, hang it up by the loop in its handle. Happy scooping!

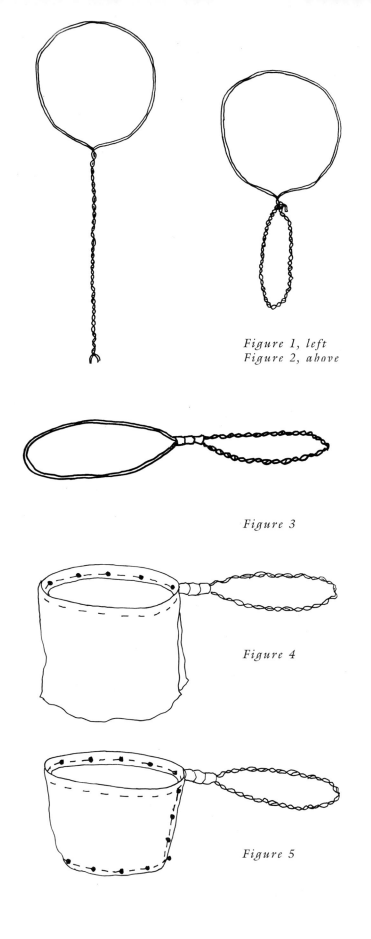

Figure 1, left
Figure 2, above

Figure 3

Figure 4

Figure 5

Water's
Skin

Most people think that water is pretty ordinary stuff, but scientists know better. Plain old water isn't plain at all. One of water's unusual properties is its strong "skin," or what scientists call *surface tension.*

You've probably noticed it when you've put too much water in a glass. Just before the water overflows, it bulges above the rim of the glass, almost as though the liquid at the top is trying to hang on for dear life.

Why? Because water molecules—the tiny particles that make up water—have an especially strong attraction for one another. They're constantly pulling inward on each other from all directions, in order to stay together. But the poor molecules at the surface don't have anything above them to hang onto except air. So they pull together more strongly on each side. And the water molecules below pull them down especially hard. The result is a kind of elastic skin of you're-not-going-anywhere water particles. Actually, all liquids have surface tension, but water's skin is tougher than most. You can even float steel on it. Fill a bowl with water, and lay a small piece of paper towel on the surface. Now, put a pin or paper clip on the towel. Then use another pin or clip to *carefully* poke the wet paper away. Presto! You've made steel float!

In nature, water's surface tension is a regular stomping ground for pond insects. Water striders and beetles skate across the surface looking for prey. And underwater, mosquito larvae hang upside down from the film, like tiny, buggy bats in a liquid cave!

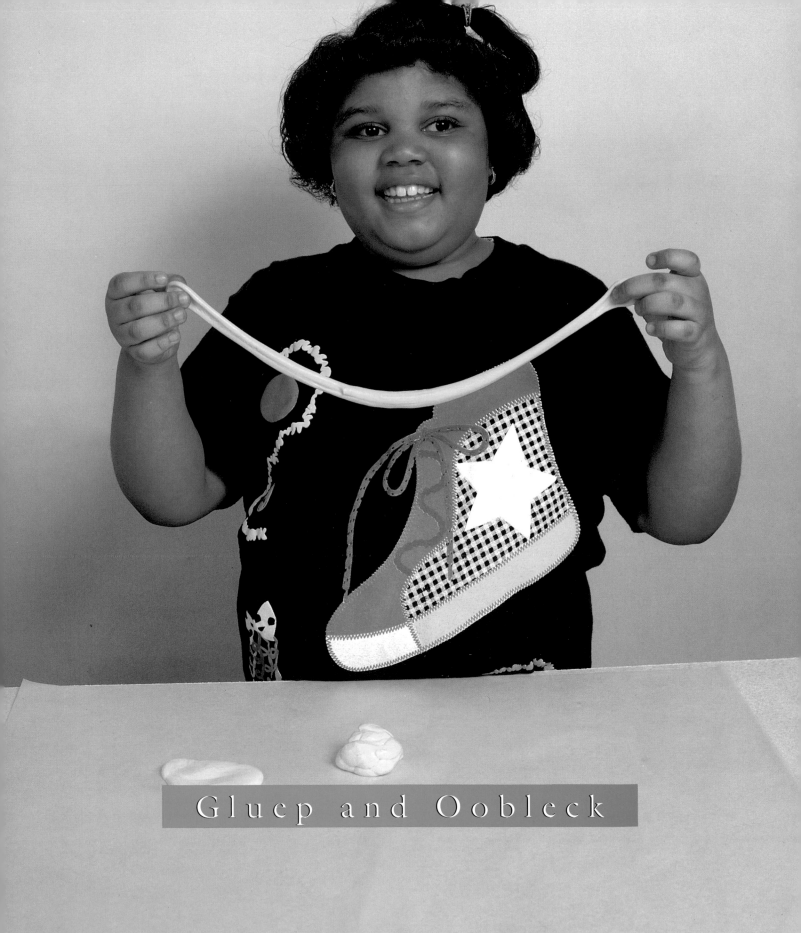

Gluep and Oobleck

"Gluep" and "oobleck" are two wonderful substances that you can make when you add water to some common household chemicals. You'll want to play with oobleck for hours! You can make up a batch of gluep to keep and play with for several days.

What You'll Need

For gluep:

Borax*

Water

Measuring spoons

2 bowls

Tacky glue or Elmer's white craft glue**

Food coloring (optional)

For oobleck:

A large bowl half filled with cornstarch

Water

*You can get borax where laundry detergents are sold.

**Don't use Sobo white glue for this project. While it's a very good craft glue, for some reason it doesn't work well in gluep.

What to Do

To make gluep:

1. Make a solution of 6 tablespoons of water and 1 teaspoon of borax. Mix the solution well.

2. In a separate bowl, mix 1 tablespoon of glue and 1 tablespoon of water. If you want colored gluep, add 1 or 2 drops of food coloring.

3. Stir a scant 2 teaspoons of the borax solution into the glue-water. Continue stirring until the mixture gets thick.

4. Knead the gluep until it's pliable. Then the fun begins! Bounce it. Stretch it. Roll it.

Pull it into a thin sheet. Pop it. Snap it. Figure out as many things to do with it as you possibly can! To save it, put it in a plastic bag in the refrigerator, so it won't dry out.

To make oobleck:

1. Simply pour water into the bowl of cornstarch. Stir the resulting mixture with your hands or a spoon.

2. Pick up a fistful of oobleck. Squeeze it. Open your hand and hold the oobleck on your palm. Roll a ball of it between your two hands to make a snake. Hold the snake by its tail and watch what happens. Try punching the oobleck in the bowl. Pick up some and rub it together until it crumbles. Pick up the crumbs and let them sit on your palm for a few seconds. See what else you can do with oobleck! You won't want to stop playing with it!

Water Lens

This simple instrument shapes clear water into a lens and lets you get a good look at small creatures and objects.

What You'll Need

An oatmeal box or other wide cylindrical cardboard container

A razor knife or other sharp knife

Plastic wrap

A heavy rubber band

Acrylic paint

A paint brush

Water

What to Do

1. Remove the lid and turn the box over. Use the knife to cut away the bottom of the box.

2. Carefully cut out three rounded shapes from the wall of the box, leaving an uncut ring at the bottom.

3. Decorate the outside of the box with acrylic paints.

4. Cut a piece of plastic wrap about 12 x 12 inches. Use the rubber band to hold the plastic wrap to the top of the box, leaving the plastic wrap loose and somewhat droopy. (This is where the water will go.)

5. Pour water in the droopy part of the plastic wrap. To use the lens, place it in a lighted area; then put the object you want to look at inside the bottom ring of the box. Peer down through the water.

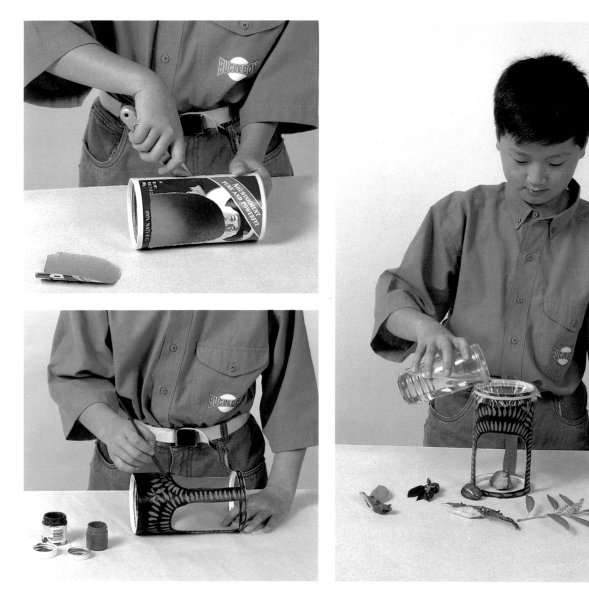

Powered Model Boats

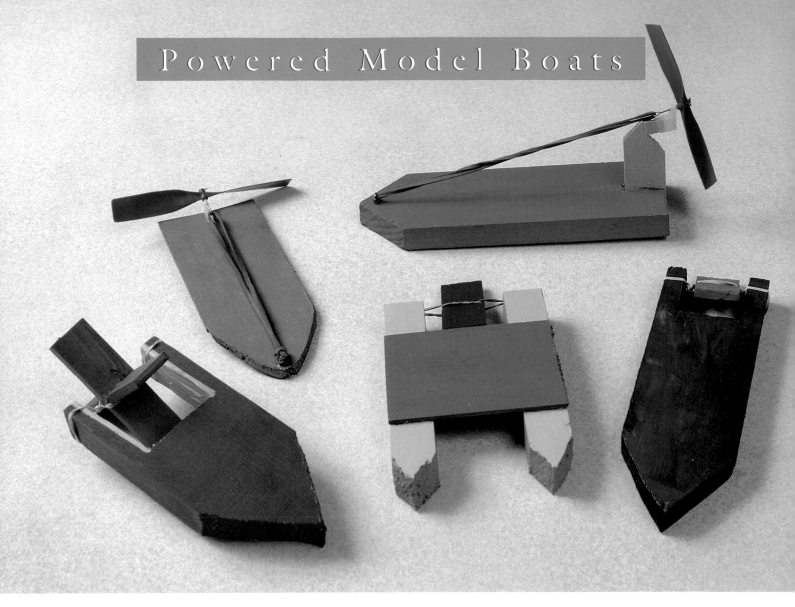

Make a flotilla of boats to help you investigate how boats move through the water. Some of these boats are powered by propellers; others move by means of paddle wheels. Once you understand the basic principles, you can invent some designs of your own.

What You'll Need

A ruler

A pencil

Pieces of lumber of assorted sizes *

A couple of wood clamps

A saw

Sandpaper

A hammer

A 1/2-inch to 1-inch wood chisel

A very narrow wood chisel

A razor knife

Carpenter's glue or balsa wood cement

Rubber bands of various sizes

Tiny screw hooks

Plastic propellers**

Acrylic paints and a brush

 *Pine and balsa both float well and are easy to work with. Balsa wood is available at craft stores.

**You can get propellers at a hobby shop that sells model airplane supplies. There are many kinds; look for the smallest and lightest ones that have plastic clips.

What to Do

1. Using the pencil and ruler, mark the lines where you want to cut the pieces of wood for hulls. Look at Figure 1 for ideas for hull shapes.

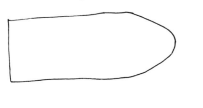

Figure 1

2. Clamp the boards to a work bench or other work surface, and saw along the lines you've drawn. Sand all cuts.

3. Cut out the places where paddles will be attached if you want to build paddle wheel boats. Cut out the propeller mount spaces if you are making propeller boats. See Figure 2.

Space for Paddle

Space for Propeller

Figure 2

To cut out these shapes, first mark them with ruler and pencil. Then make the saw cuts from point A to point B and from point C to point D. To cut line B-D, hammer the chisel along the line you've drawn. This will give you a shallow cut.

Deepen the cut by hammering over the line some more. When the line is about 1/8 inch deep, hammer inward from the end of the hull toward line B-D. See Figure 3. Pieces of wood should lift up. Remove these pieces of wood, and then hammer another, deeper line from point B to

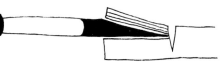

Figure 3

point D. Continue to hammer line B-D and then chisel up from the end of the hull to the line until the entire space is cleared out. See Figure 4.

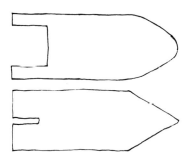

Figure 4

4. Cut out paddle wheels and paddles with a razor knife or saw, depending on the kind of wood you are using. Balsa wood cuts easily with a knife if it is thin enough. See Figure 5 for shapes.

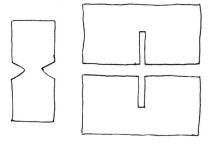

Figure 5

5. If you are using some paddle wheels, assemble them as in Figure 6.

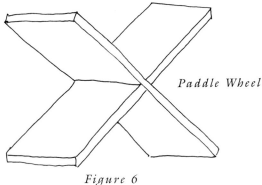

Paddle Wheel

Figure 6

6. Cut out propeller mounts if you are using propellers. See Figure 7.

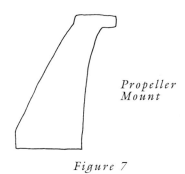

Propeller Mount

Figure 7

7. Assemble the boats. Tie rubber bands into thirds. Slip the two end loops over hull points, and slip the paddle or paddle wheel into the middle loop. See Figure 8. Mount propellers as in Figure 9.

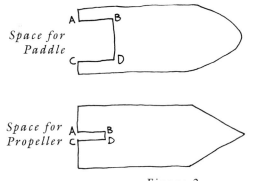

Figure 8

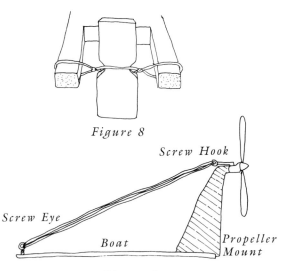

Screw Hook

Screw Eye

Boat

Propeller Mount

Figure 9

8. Paint the boats with acrylic paint. When the paint has dried completely, test out your fleet. You'll notice some interesting things about what happens when you spin a propeller in different directions. What other discoveries can you make? What other designs can you dream up?

Try This Puzzle!
(Water You Weighting For?)

The two glasses you see here are identical. They're both full right up to the rim with water. But one has a block of wood floating in it. If you weighed each of the glasses, which would be heaviest?

Answer: First read "What Makes a Boat Float" on page 109 and see if you can guess.

(Okay…the answer is at the bottom of page 109.)

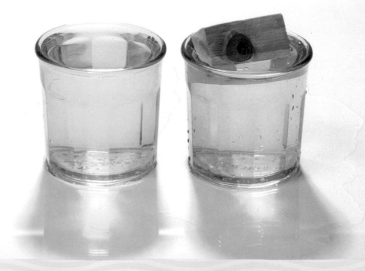

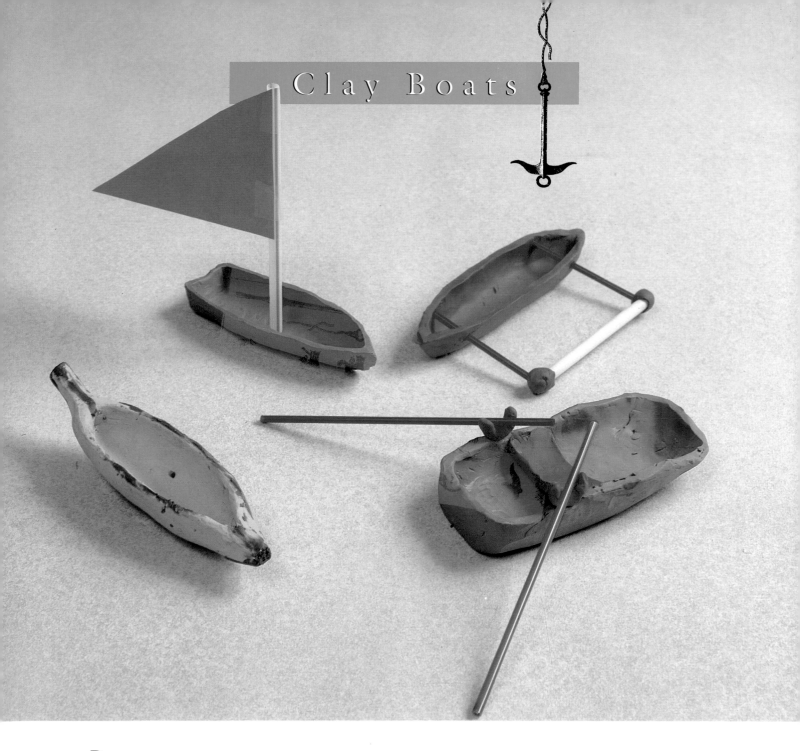

Drop a ball of clay into a tub of water, and watch it sink like a stone. Now shape the ball of clay into a boat, and watch it float! What's going on here? In this project, you'll make some discoveries about when and why clay can float.

What You'll Need

A tub of water

Modeling clay (also called plasticine clay—NOT pottery clay)

Small sticks (toothpicks or matchsticks)

Small pieces of paper

Scissors

An awl or large nail

Tools to help form clay, such as plastic knives and spoons

What to Do

1. Fill the tub with water. Spend some time playing with different clay shapes to learn which shapes float best.

2. Form different shapes of boats. You might try a canoe, a double-hulled catamaran, an outrigger canoe (with matchsticks held together by small beads of clay to form the outrigger), sailboats, and ships with enclosed, hollow hulls. Test all of your boats.

3. As you begin to discover which shapes float best, refine your designs. Build the biggest boat you can that will float; build the smallest. Make sails out of paper with matchstick masts.

4. Look at the boats in the photograph. Which designs do you think will float? Which are probably sinkers?

5. Here are some hints. Plasticine will get gooey after a few minutes in the water, so it's best to let your boats dry out before smashing them and reworking them. You can wash plasticine off of your hands with dish detergent and water. Gooey-wet plasticine will dry out and be as good as new after an hour or so.

What Makes a *Boat Float?*

If you throw a chunk of steel into water, it sinks like a rock. But if you weld 600,000 tons of steel into the shape of a supertanker, it floats. How can that be?

Whether a boat, a cork, a rock, your Uncle Bill, or anything else floats depends on two things: how much it weighs, and how big it is. Scientists call those two things—the heaviness of an object for its size—*density*.

When you put something in water, it pushes down on the water with as much force as its own weight. And it shoves aside—or *displaces*—enough water to make room for itself.

If the object isn't any heavier than the amount of water it shoves aside, no problem. It floats. The liquid that was holding up the water supports the object instead. But if the what-ever-it-is weighs more than the water it displaces, it sinks.

A chunk of metal sinks because it's a lot heavier than the little bit of water it pushes aside. The liquid that was holding up that little bit of water can't possibly hold up the metal.

A 1,000-foot-long, 200-foot-wide, 600,000-ton steel supertanker is a different story. It floats because it's not only heavy, it's *big*. And it isn't solid. There are lots of rooms full of air, which weighs almost nothing.

When a supertanker is launched, it sinks down until the amount of water it pushes aside (and it pushes a *lot* of water) equals the weight of the ship. The rest of the ship floats above the surface. Whene cargo is loaded, weight is added and the ship sinks a little lower. But as long as the boat and cargo weigh less than the water the ship is pushing aside, it will float.

As for your Uncle Bill: He can float in a lake or pool—but not in a bathtub. Why? Because in a pool, there's enough room for Uncle Bill to push his own weight in water out of the way and still have plenty of water left beneath to support him. But in a tub, there's probably not enough water for Uncle Bill to push aside his weight, and certainly not enough left underneath to hold him up. So he sinks.

Answer to puzzle on page 106: In order to float, the block of wood had to push aside its own weight in water. That water spilled over the edge of the glass. So the weight of the two glasses is the same.

FIRE—

the heart and soul of our sun.
That blazing ball of fire is the center
of all life on Earth, the source of heat
and light. Use the sun as we humans
have always done. Arrange some stones
into a solar clock to help you track
the seasons, as ancient people did at
Stonehenge....Cook your food in a solar
oven, and preserve it in a solar dryer....
Grow some plants in a tiny green-
house....Then play with the sun's light—
make color spinners and light catchers....
Find your way by the sun's light, just as
your ancestors did—make a solar stone,
an astrolabe, a cross staff....Finally,
look at other, more distant suns with
your star magnitude gauge.

FIRE

Solar Clock

Early people watched the sky more than most of us do today. They watched movements of the sun, moon, and stars that many of us never notice. Some people even developed gigantic sky clocks that helped them keep track of changing seasons. Stonehenge in southern England is thought to be one of these.

For ancient people in the northern hemisphere, the summer solstice was a very important time of the year. It was the time when the sun was most directly overhead and the days were longest. Plants grew strongest at this time of year. It was a time of great feasting and ceremony. It was important to know when the solstice was coming.

In this project, you will make a small solar clock that will help you learn to notice some important movements of the sun.

What You'll Need

A large, shallow dish, such as a dish that goes under a very large clay or plastic flowerpot

Soil to fill the dish

A trowel

7 pointy-topped rocks, each one about 2 to 3 inches tall

A calendar

Mosses (optional)

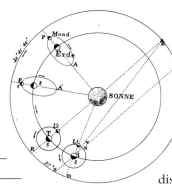

What to Do

1. You'll have to begin this project at a certain time of year. The equinoxes—the days when night and day are of equal length—are around March 21 and September 21. The summer solstice—the day when the sun is in the sky for the longest period all year (if you live in the northern hemisphere)—is around June 21. The winter solstice—the shortest day of the year in the northern hemisphere—is around December 21. You should begin this project at one of these times: March 18 or 19, June 18 or 19, September 18 or 19, December 18 or 19.

2. The most important step in this project is finding the right location for your clock. You need a place from which you can see both sunrise and sunset all year round. It's best if you can see the distant horizon, the place where the sky and land seem to touch each other. If the sun sets behind trees or mountains where you live, you can still make a solar clock, but it will work best if you can see a distant horizon.

3. Once you've settled on a place, set up a stand for the dish. This should be something sturdy, such as a table or plant stand, and it should be high enough that you can see the setting sun when you look across the dish at eye level. If you think the stand and dish might be disturbed from time to time during the year, make a mark on the side of the dish and on the table so that you can reposition the dish if someone should move it.

4. Place the dish on the table or stand, and fill it with soil. Place a rock on top of the soil in the exact center of the dish. We'll call this your *center stone.*

5. On one of the four dates, go outside in the evening at sunset. Find the place on the near edge of the dish from which you can look directly at the sun across the center rock. Place a rock just inside the rim to mark this spot. We will call this your *spotting stone.*

6. Place a second rock inside the rim nearest the setting sun as you look from your spotting stone across the center rock. This is your *rim stone.* See Figure 1.

7. On the next evening, go outside and again look at the setting sun from your spotting stone across the center stone. Move the rim stone if you need to so that it lines up with the setting sun. You probably won't notice much change, if any, but it's a good idea to check your placement.

8. Continue checking the placement of the rim stone until the solstice or equinox has passed. Another reason to start checking a few days before the actual date is to increase your

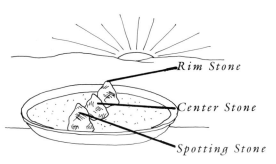

Rim Stone

Center Stone

Spotting Stone

Figure 1

chances of catching at least one sunset in case there are some cloudy days around the event. The actual date of the event should be on a calendar.

9. Watch your calendar until a few days before the next big solar event—equinox or solstice—and repeat Steps 5, 6, 7, and 8. Be sure to place the dish in the same position each time. You'll notice that you will need to place a new spotting stone as well as a new rim stone.

10. Repeat the process for the next two solar events.

11. Here are a couple of interesting facts that you may want to check by getting up early enough to view a sunrise.

The spotting stone for the winter solstice sunset will be the rim stone for the summer solstice sunrise; the rim stone for the winter solstice sunset will be the spotting stone for the summer solstice sunrise.

The spotting stone for the summer solstice sunset will be the rim stone for the winter solstice sunrise; the rim stone for the summer solstice sunset will be the spotting stone for the winter solstice sunrise! What can you discover about the equinox stones?

12. If you want to, decorate your clock by planting mosses around the stones.

The Sun,
Center of Life

Most of us don't give the sun much thought. It rises in the morning, sets in the evening, and makes summer days hot, right?

Right. But it also keeps us alive. All life on Earth depends entirely on the sun. In fact, without the sun life never would have existed here.

The sun's gravity holds Earth and all the other planets in our solar system in orbit. Its light gives green plants the energy to grow and produce oxygen for us to breathe. Its heat drives the winds, rains, and ocean currents. The sun provides food for us to eat and gives us the materials we use to build our homes and clothe ourselves. The fuel we use to drive our cars and heat our houses contains the sun's energy. Wood blazing in a fireplace gives off the power of sunlight stored by a growing tree. The energy in oil, gas, and coal is the sun's, captured millions of years ago by plants and animals.

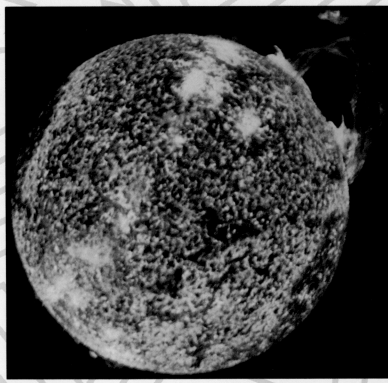

Everything about the sun is as dazzling as the star itself.

☛ The sun weighs as much as 332,946 planets the size of Earth.

☛ More than one million Earths could fit inside the sun!

☛ The sun is about 4-1/2 billion years old. Scien-tists say it will last at least another five billion years.

☛ Gravity is much more powerful on the sun than on Earth. If you weighed 100 pounds on Earth, you'd weigh 2,800 pounds on the sun!

☛ The sun is about 93 million miles from Earth. If you decided to travel to the sun, you'd be in for a long trip. It would take about 193 years to get there in a car going 55 mph. You'd get there a little sooner if you took a 100-mile-an-hour express train, though: just 106 years. A Boeing 737 going 450 miles an hour would make the trip in 24 years. Even a spaceship traveling at 25,000 miles an hour would have to fly more than five months to get to the sun!

☛ The sun is our nearest star. If the thickness of this page stood for the distance between Earth and the sun, the distance between Earth and the next nearest star would be a stack of paper 71 feet tall!

☛ It takes only about eight minutes for light and heat from the sun to reach Earth.

☛ The temperature of the sun's core is 27 million degrees Fahrenheit (15 million degrees Centigrade). In just one second the sun gives off more energy than people have used since the beginning of mankind.

Solar Oven

This is the simplest design for a solar oven that you are likely to find anywhere. All of the materials are things you can easily find. On a bright, sunny day, you can bake a batch of cookies in your oven while your family and friends watch in amazement!

What You'll Need

2 cardboard grocery boxes*

A razor knife

White craft glue

A bowl to mix glue and water

A 1- or 2-inch-wide soft paint brush

About 2 rolls of large-size aluminum foil

Scissors

A flat piece of cardboard 7 inches longer and 7 inches wider than the length and width of the outer box

Several other flat pieces of cardboard the same size as, or larger

than, the walls of the inner box

2 large, clear plastic, turkey-roasting bags

Paper tape (the kind that you have to wet in order to make it stick)

Self-adhesive shelf paper

A stick about the same length as the width of the outer box

An aluminum cookie sheet or oven bottom liner

A can of flat black latex spray paint

*The ideal inner box is 19 by 23 by 8 inches. The ideal outer box is a little wider, longer, and taller: 23 by 27 by 9 inches. If you can't find these exact sizes, look for an inner box that fits inside the outer box with about an inch of space on all sides and the bottom. Boxes that are bigger than the ideal are better than boxes that are smaller; rectangular boxes are better than square ones. The inner box should be as shallow as possible, but taller than the pots you will use. The pots can't touch the window.

What to Do

1. Cut the flaps off the inner box. Leave the flaps on the outer box.

2. Pour about a cup of glue into the bowl, and add about the same amount of water. Stir well. Using the paint brush to apply the glue, glue aluminum foil to the entire inside and outside surfaces of the inner box and to the entire inside surface of the outer box. Also cover both sides of the flaps on the outer box. Do your best to keep the aluminum foil smooth.

3. Cut little pieces of card-board 1 inch by 1 inch. You will need enough to make six stacks, each of them 1 inch tall. Glue the pieces together to make the six stacks. Glue the stacks to the inside bottom of the outer box. See Figure 1.

4. Put a bit of glue on the top of each stack, and carefully place the inner box on the stacks. Arrange it so that there is about 1 inch of space between the four walls of the inner box and the four walls of the outer box. See Figure 2.

5. Cut flat pieces of cardboard to fit in the spaces between the walls of the two boxes. These

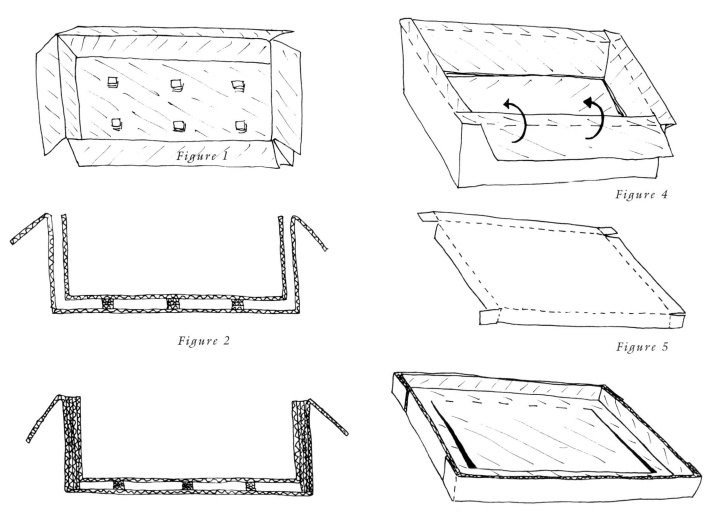

Figure 1

Figure 2

Figure 3

Figure 4

Figure 5

Figure 6

pieces will be the insulation. Glue aluminum foil to one side of each flat piece. When the glue has dried, slip the flat pieces into the spaces between the box walls. Face the shiny side toward the outside. When all the pieces of insulation are in place, the inner box should fit snugly inside the outer box. See Figure 3.

6. Fold the flaps of the outer box up and around the inner box walls. Trim the flaps to fit. These flaps should be covered with aluminum foil on both sides. See Figure 4.

7. Glue the flaps in place.

8. Glue foil to one side of the large flat piece of cardboard that you will use for the lid. Center this piece of cardboard over the boxes, foil side down. Fold the edges over the finished box for a good fit. Cut and fold corner flaps and glue them. See Figure 5.

9. Remove the lid, and place it inside up on a table or the floor. Draw a window opening in the center of the lid the size of the opening of the inner box. Be sure this opening is a little smaller than the turkey roasting bag.

10. Cut three sides of the window, leaving one long side to fold up for a reflector. See Figure 6.

11. Spread glue along the edge of the window frame and stretch the turkey roasting bags in the opening. (You will be using four layers of plastic.) Pull the bags tight so that the plastic stretches smoothly across the window opening.

12. Replace the lid on the oven. Open the reflector lid. Trim the stick so that it is the

right length to prop open the lid at different angles.

13. Completely cover the outside of the box and lid with self-adhesive paper.

14. Spray-paint the aluminum cookie sheet black, and allow it to dry.

15. To use the oven, place it outdoors in a sunny spot. Place the black sheet in the bottom of the oven. Mix cookies according to your favorite recipe, and place them on a dark aluminum or nonstick baking sheet. Put the baking sheet on the black cookie sheet on the floor of the oven.

If your oven seems too deep for the cookies, place a couple of aluminum pie pans upside

down on the black cookie sheet, and place the baking sheet of cookies on them. That way, the cookies will be closer to the window. Place the lid on the oven. Angle the oven so that the sun shines directly into the center of the box. Adjust the reflector angle to focus sunlight in the oven. It will take several hours to bake the cookies, depending on how warm the day is and how bright the sun is. Check on the oven from time to time, and adjust the angle of the oven and of the reflector to keep the sun shining inside the oven. Don't open the lid until you think the cookies are done, as heat will quickly escape once you open it. Use a hot pad to handle the cookie pan. It will get very hot! Your solar oven will heat up to about 275 degrees F on a hot, sunny day when there are many hours of sunlight.

16. Experiment with cooking other things in your oven. Here are some hints: Put food into dark-colored, covered pots (although cookies don't need to be covered). If you are cooking fresh vegetables, don't add water. For other foods, start with the recipe you usually use, and adjust it if it isn't cooking right. Smaller pots of food will cook faster. The thinner the sides of the pot, the faster the food will cook. Small pieces of food will cook faster than large ones.

Polar
Solar Collectors

You've probably heard of solar collectors—devices that "catch" the sun's warmth and use it to heat water or even an entire house. If you live in a sunny part of the planet, your home may have a solar collector. It's probably up on the roof, where it can be aimed at the sun to capture the most heat.

But did you know that one of the world's best "solar collectors" isn't manmade at all, and works even in the coldest places on Earth? This solar collector has fur, four legs, and weighs over 1,000 pounds. It's a polar bear!

Polar bear hairs are like tiny, see-through pipes. They're hollow and completely transparent. The fur only looks white to us because the inside wall of each hollow hair reflects visible light—the part of sunlight we can see. But the hairs also do something else. They trap ultraviolet light—one of the parts of sunshine that we *can't* see. Ultraviolet light is the invisible energy that gives people suntans.

The bear's hollow hairs grab the ultraviolet radiation and lead it, like hot water in a pipe, to the animal's skin—which, under all that fur, is black. Black absorbs solar energy. So the bear soaks up the sun's energy like a sponge and stays warm in weather that would give almost any other creature the cold shivers. Manmade solar collectors have to be pointed at the sun to make them grab as much heat as possible. But polar bear fur traps light coming from any direction. And the animals lose very little heat, because the hairs are strictly one-way: Ultraviolet energy can flow toward the animal's skin, but never away from it.

No wonder solar engineers are studying polar bears! They're trying to figure out how to use the bear-hair's heat-catching tricks in manmade designs. Who knows? Maybe someday all solar collectors will be white and fuzzy!

119

This food dryer will let you preserve food for later…or turn your favorite fruits into handy snacks.

What You'll Need

A cardboard box about 12 by 16 by 24 inches, open at one end

A razor knife

Aluminum foil

Cellophane tape

Black plastic tape about an inch wide

Clear plastic wrap or a clear plastic paint drop cloth

About a yard of vinyl window screen cloth or cheesecloth

1 or 2 cake cooling racks

Acrylic paints

A paint brush

What to Do

1. Lay the box down on one of its large sides.

2. Make a cut from the top corner of the open end of the box straight along the edge until the cut is about 2 inches from the closed end of the box. Make an identical cut along the other top edge. See Figure 1.

3. "Score" a line between points A and B on Figure 2. (Score means to cut just deeply enough to leave a groove. DON'T cut all the way through the cardboard.) The top of the box should now bend easily to a slant, touching the bottom of the box. See Figure 2.

4. Trim the sides of the box so that they follow the slant of the top. See Figure 3. Trim off any flaps that stick out on the bottom past the place where the slanting top touches the bottom.

5. Carefully cut three windows, one in each side and one on the slanting top of the box. Leave a frame about 1-1/2 inches wide around each window. See Figure 4.

6. Cut pieces of aluminum foil big enough to line the inside bottom, back, and sides of the box. Tape the foil in place with loops or strips of cellophane tape.

7. Cut out two triangles of screen or cheesecloth slightly larger than the two side windows.

8. Tape the screen or cheesecloth to the outside of the windows with black plastic tape.

9. Cut a piece of plastic slightly larger than the slanted top opening. If you need to, use cellophane tape to tape two smaller pieces together to get a big enough piece.

10. Stretch and tape the plastic to the outside of the top window, using black plastic tape. See Figure 5. The entire frame—top and sides—should now be covered with black tape.

11. Paint the top and back of the box with black acrylic paint. If you want to add some designs to the box, do that now, but be sure to leave most of the box black so that it will absorb heat more readily.

12. Place the oven racks inside the food dryer. To use the dryer, lay thinly sliced fruit or vegetables (apples, sweet potatoes, pears, apricots) on the racks. Close the dryer and place it in a sunny spot indoors or outdoors. The fruit will dry in 10 days to two weeks, depending on how dry the weather is. If you place the dryer outside, be sure to bring it in at night or in rainy weather.

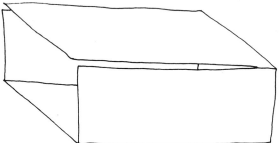

Figure 1

Figure 2

Figure 3

Figure 4

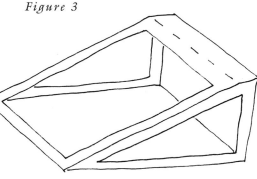

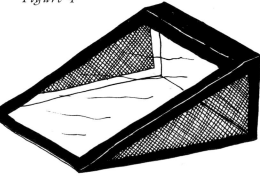

Figure 5

This mini-greenhouse will keep plants warm and cozy all winter long. If you put it in a sunny spot, you'll be able to pick lettuce for a salad in January! In spring, you can simply lift up the tepee and fold its legs together for easy storage.

What You'll Need

3 pieces of edge molding, each 36 inches long*

Enamel spray paint

A hammer

A nail

3 screw eyes**

4 inches of soft wire

A permanent marker

Scissors

Clear plastic (either an old shower curtain or a heavy plastic paint drop cloth)

A staple gun

3 clothespins

*Edge molding is a kind of lumber that is cut to wrap around edges of walls. If you look at the end of a piece, it will be curved (see Figure 1). You can buy edge molding at a large hardware store or a lumberyard.

Figure 1   *Figure 2*

**A screw eye is a small ring attached to a screw (see Figure 2), available at hardware stores and discount marts.

What to Do

1. Spray-paint the three pieces of edge molding completely.

2. After they're dry, use the hammer and nail to make a starter hole in one end of each of the sticks.

3. Place a screw eye in each starter hole, and screw it in with your fingers. (Or thread the nail through the screw hole, and turn it like a faucet to tighten it.)

4. Tie the three screw eyes loosely together with the wire. See Figure 3.

5. Spread the three pieces of wood to form a triangular framework around your plants. Push the ends of the sticks into the ground, about an inch deep, to anchor them. Make sure that the 1/4-inch edge of the molding is facing outward

on the piece that will be the door. The clothespins will then be able to grip that edge.

6. Use markers and scissors to cut three triangular pieces of plastic to fit over the three sides. Leave about an inch of extra plastic on each edge for stapling to the framework.

7. Ask a grown-up to help you staple two of the triangular pieces of plastic to the frame. Then staple ONE SIDE only of the third piece, leaving one side open for a door.

8. Use clothespins to fasten the loose side when you want the door closed. Open the door and clothespin it back on warm days.

9. If you live in a place where the winters are very cold, use two layers of plastic for all of the walls of the tepee.

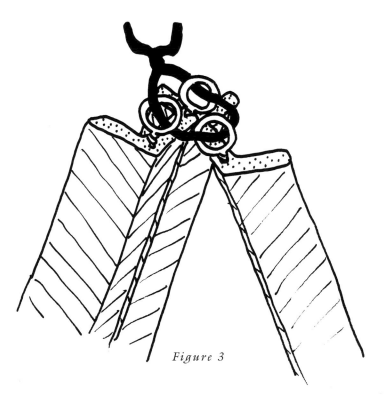

Figure 3

Color Spinners

When you spin these, you'll see colors change in front of your eyes as if by magic!

What You'll Need

Corrugated cardboard (such as the flaps from an old box)

Something round to use as a pattern to draw a circle (such as a quart-sized paint can or an upside down bowl)

A pencil

A razor knife

A piece of 1/4-inch dowel, about 7 inches long for each spinner

Red, blue, and yellow acrylic paints

A brush

A saw

A pencil sharpener (optional)

An awl or a large nail

What to Do

1. Tracing around your pattern, draw a circle about 4 inches in diameter on the cardboard.

2 Cut the circle out, using the razor knife.

3. Paint the circle, using two of the colors. Paint pie-shaped wedges in alternating colors, until you completely fill in the circle. (The easiest way to make wedges is to draw straight lines across the circle so that they all cross exactly in the center.)

4. Use the awl or nail to poke a starter hole in the exact center of the cardboard circle.

5. Saw off a 7-inch-long piece of dowel, and sharpen one end either with the razor knife or in a pencil sharpener.

6. Poke the sharpened end of the dowel through the hole in the center of the circle. Push about 3 inches of the dowel through the hole.

7. To spin the spinner, make a loose circle with the fingers of one hand, and slip the pointy (bottom) end of the spinner dowel through the hole in your hands. Rest the pointy end on a table top or the floor. Use your other hand to spin the top of the dowel. Loosely support the bottom of the spinner with your bottom hand while you continue to spin the spinner with your other hand. Watch what happens to the colors.

8. Make other spinners using other combinations of colors. Try making one with all three colors. Try using white and a color or black and a color. Experiment!

124

Mixed-Up
Colors

Magenta   Yellow   Cyan

Have you ever painted with watercolors? Then you probably know that if you mix blue paint and yellow paint, you get green paint. But wait a minute. If you shine a blue light and a yellow light together, you get *white*. Why?

Colored lights and colored paints mix completely differently. Paints, inks, and dyes contain *pig-*

ments that soak up all the colors of the rainbow except the ones they reflect. For example, blue paint absorbs all of the spectrum except blue.

Every time you mix two colored paints together, you make a paint that absorbs more of the spectrum than before. The new color is always a little closer to black, which of course doesn't reflect any color at all.

The primary colors for pigments are yellow, cyan (pronounced SY-ann—a greenish blue), and magenta (purple-red). Printers and painters mix yellow, cyan, and magenta inks or paints to make all of their colors.

Mixing colored light is the opposite of mixing paints. White light contains all the colors of the spectrum. So every time you combine one colored light with another, you make a color that's a little closer to white.

The primary colors for light are red, green, and blue. By mixing just those three colors of light in different amounts, you can make any color in the world. Scientists say it's possible to create more than a million distinct colors of light!

For one example of how people use light's primary colors, check out a color TV screen. Look very closely, or through a magnifying glass. (Don't hurt your eyes. Look for just a few seconds.) Surprise! All of the colors on the screen are actually made up of thousands of tiny red, blue, and green stripes or dots.

The color spinners on page 124 can help you understand the ways colors mix. Try making a blue and yellow color spinner. If the two paints happen to overlap a bit where the wedges meet, they'll combine to make a greenish color. That's because you mixed their pigments and created a paint that absorbs more of the spectrum. But when you spin the spinner, you combine the blue and yellow *light* reflecting off the card. The moving spinner looks white. Likewise, if you make a red and green spinner, any mixed-up paint will be blackish. But when you spin the card, the red and blue reflected light combine to make yellow!

125

The ancient Chinese made clocks that worked by burning a candle. This fire clock uses an incense stick instead of a candle, so it will smell sweet as it helps you tell time.

What to Do

1. Make a simple figure out of the clay, such as a bird, a person, or an animal standing on its hind legs. Or simply shape the clay into a cylinder or wedge. The figure or shape should be about 3 inches tall.

2. Push the handle of a stick of incense into the figure's mouth or somewhere else near the top. Be sure the stick is held firm, with about 1 inch of it sticking into the clay. The stick should slant slightly upward.

3. Stand the figure with the incense stick at one end of the heat-proof dish. The stick should reach across to the other side of the dish but not stick over the edge.

4. Cut pieces of thread about 4 inches long. Tie a jingle bell to each end so that you have five or six pairs of bells on strings.

5. Ask an adult to help you light the stick of incense. Drape a pair of bells over the incense stick about 1 inch down from the lighted tip. Use a watch or clock to see how long it takes for the stick to burn to the thread. When the burning tip reaches the thread, it will burn through it, and the bells will drop to the dish, making a tinkling sound. After you've seen how long it takes the incense to burn a certain distance—for example, 1 inch—you can place the other pairs of bells along the stick at the spaces you want. You might want a pair of bells to drop every 15 minutes. Or you might want to use the clock to time something that needs to go on for an hour. Experiment with extra sticks of incense. You'll soon figure out how to set your clock to go off when you want it to.

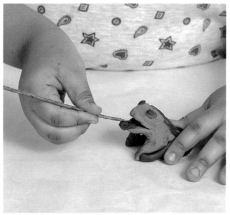

What You'll Need

A ball of plasticine clay (modeling clay) the size of your fist

Several sticks of incense

A flat, heat-proof dish or tray (such as an aluminum baking pan)

Thread

Scissors

About 10 small jingle bells

A clock or watch

A match

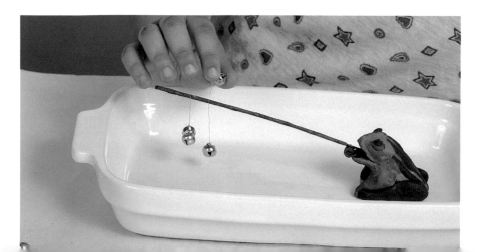

Dried Apple Garland

After you've built a solar food dryer (see page 120), you can make a dried apple garland with some of the slices your dryer turns out. Experiment with making other kinds of garlands, too. You might try dried sweet potato slices with raisins (dried grapes), or pears and pineapple spears.

What You'll Need

Raffia*

A big-eyed needle

Dried apple slices

Whole cranberries or other firm, edible berries

*Raffia is sold in craft stores.

What to Do

1. Thread the needle with a thick strand of raffia. Tie a big knot about 2 inches from the end of the strand.

2. Poke the needle through either a cranberry or an apple end slice (if you have one).

3. Thread apple slices and cranberries until you run out of apple slices. Finish off with either a cranberry or another apple end slice.

4. Tie a loop in the end of the raffia and cut off the rest of it.

5. Hang the garland in a dry, shady place, and snack off it until all that's left is the raffia.

Light Catcher

When you join 12 five-sided figures, called pentagons, to form a three-dimensional solid, the solid is called a dodecahedron (doh-dek-uh-HEE-dron). If you cover the 12 surfaces of a dodecahedron with shiny paper, it will gather and reflect light and fill your room with pieces of the rainbow.

What You'll Need

A piece of heavy paper, such as lightweight poster board or bristol board

Tracing paper

Carbon paper

A sharp pencil

Sharp scissors or a razor knife

A ruler or straightedge

A table knife

Rubber cement

Pieces of shiny paper, such as wrapping paper or foil

Dental floss or monofilament fishing line

A needle

What to Do

1. Make a template from one of the shapes given in Figure 1. Choose either the large or the

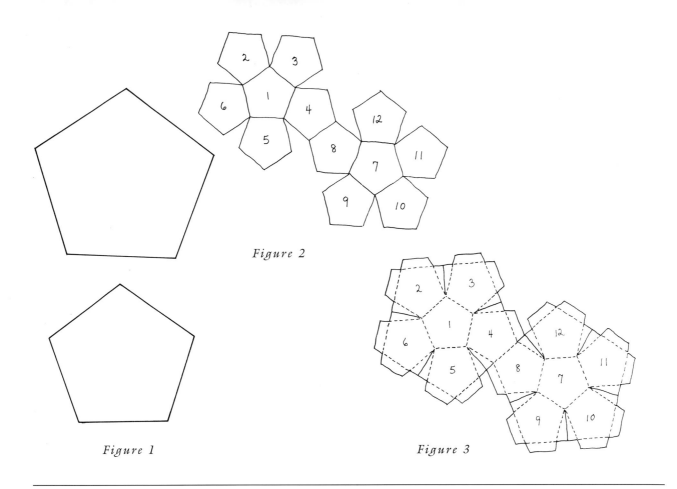

Figure 2

Figure 1

Figure 3

small shape, but use the same shape for all of the pentagons of each dodecahedron.

To make a template, trace the shape onto tracing paper. Use a ruler to make sure the lines are perfectly straight. Then put a piece of carbon paper between the tracing paper and a piece of heavy paper, with the carbon side facing the heavy paper. Draw over the figure you have traced. You should now have a copy of the shape on heavy paper. Carefully cut out this shape, making sure all lines are perfectly straight.

2. Use the template to draw the pentagons as shown in Figure 2. Notice that each pentagon shares at least one edge with another pentagon. The numbers in Figure 2 are to help

you keep track. You do not need to write the numbers on your drawing.

3. Draw the tabs as shown by the solid lines in Figure 3.

4. With sharp scissors or a razor knife, carefully cut out the figure. Be sure to cut ONLY along the outside of the tabs. Do NOT cut the tabs off the figure.

5. Using the table knife, score all of the lines between pentagons and between pentagons and tabs. (These are the dotted lines in Figure 3.) To score lines, place a ruler along the line and draw a table knife along the line so that the line is pressed down but not cut. Scoring a line makes it easier to fold.

6. Carefully fold all the tabs down in the same direction.

Then fold all the outer pentagons down. Fold the line between the two units of pentagons so that the two units face each other.

7. Put rubber cement on the top surface of each tab. Let it dry. (It will look dull when it is dry.) When the cement is dry, press the tabs that are next to each other together, causing the two groups of pentagons to come together and form angular bowls, as in Figure 4. Be careful as you press the tabs together, because once dry rubber-cemented surfaces are joined, they can't be pulled apart.

8. Now join the two bowls by pressing together the tabs that face each other on the two units. Again, be careful, because dry rubber cement can't be moved.

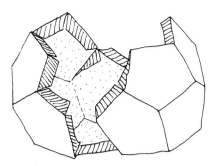

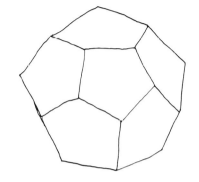

Figure 4

9. You now have a dodeca-hedron, but not a light catch-er. To make a light catcher, use the template that you made to draw pentagons on shiny paper or foil. Cut out each shiny pentagon. Coat each pentagon on the dodec-ahedron with rubber cement, and coat the back of each shiny paper pentagon with rubber cement. When the cement has dried, press the shiny pentagons onto the dodecahedron.

10. Thread a needle with dental floss or monofilament. Pierce a small hole in the cor-ner of one shiny pentagon, and pull the floss through. Tie a knot to hold the floss in place. Hang the dodecahe-dron in a sunny window.

Light *and Color*

When you hear the word *reflection,* you probably think of what you see when you look in a mirror. But actually, almost *everything* you see is a reflection of light bouncing off an object and into your eyes. Have you ever been in a super-dark place? A place so dark you couldn't see your own hand when you held it in front of your face? Your hand was there, of course. But you couldn't see it because there was no light reflecting from it.

Light from the sun or some other source is called *white* light, but it is really a mixture of seven colors: red, orange, yellow, green, blue, indigo, and violet. These make up the spectrum—the colors you see in a rainbow. The seven colors usually travel together, combined as white light, until they are reflected by something. Then the light rays bounce back into our eyes.

But not all objects reflect all the colors back in equal amounts. Some things absorb part of the spectrum and reflect only what's left. That's why our world is such a colorful and interesting place. When you look at a green leaf, you're seeing the green part of white light reflected by the leaf. The other colors have been absorbed by the leaf. When sunlight strikes a red rose, the flower "soaks up" all the colors in the spectrum except red, which it bounces back into your eyes. The polka dots on Uncle Fred's tie are white because they reflect all the colors in light. The black background of the tie is black because it soaks up all the colors. And that little yellow spot of spilled mustard is there because it reflects the yellow part of the spectrum—and because Uncle Fred is a sloppy eater!

Solar Stone

The Vikings had a simple stone or wooden instrument called a solar stone, or bearing dial, that helped them find north, which was home for the Vikings. You can use your solar stone to navigate around your neighborhood or when you're exploring new territory. It can also help you find your way around the sky at night.

What You'll Need

A piece of corrugated cardboard about 5 by 5 inches

Something to use as a pattern to draw a circle with a 4-inch diameter

A pencil

A razor knife

A straight-sided cork

A 5-inch length of 1-inch-diameter dowel

A hacksaw

Super glue

An awl or a large nail

Two 1-1/2-inch-long finishing nails (They have very small heads.)

Acrylic paints and a brush

A permanent black marker or puffy plastic paint in a squeeze bottle

What to Do

1. Make the dial by tracing a 4-inch circle onto the cardboard and then cutting it out with the razor knife.

2. Find the exact center of the circle, and center one end of the cork over that spot. Now trace around the cork. Carefully cut out this small circle. Test the size of the small circle by sliding the cork into it. If the

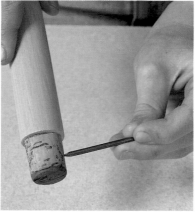

design, make four points for the four directions—north, south, east, and west. Use black marker or puffy paint to label the four directions.

8. Paint the handle, including the cork.

9. Assemble the solar stone by sliding the dial over the cork. Then push a finishing nail into the top hole and one into the side hole.

10. You can use the solar stone both during the day and at night to find north. Here's what you do. Go outside at noon and point the side nail, or pointer stick, in the direction in which you are walking. Now hold the stone so that the top nail, or shadow stick, casts a shadow on the dial. Turn the dial so that "north" lines up with the shadow. Since the sun's shadow points north at noon in the northern hemisphere (line the shadow up with "south" if you live in the southern hemisphere), you can tell the direction in which you are heading, as well as other directions.

At night, set the pointer stick so that it points in the direction in which you are heading, then hold the dial at eye level so that you can sight the North, or polar, Star with the shadow stick. You may have to turn around until you find the star. When you find the star and are able to sight it, turn the dial so that north points in the direction of the star. You can now read the direction that the pointer stick is pointing. That is the direction in which you are heading. You can also read where north, south, east, and west are.

This instrument works best in the far north. Why might that be?

cork won't go in easily, gently enlarge the circle by trimming away a little cardboard equally around the circle.

3. Saw off a 5-inch length of dowel.

4. Saw the cork in half. Be very careful to make a straight cut so that the cork will stand flat on its cut end.

5. Glue the sawn end of the cork to one end of the dowel.

6. After the glue is dry, use the awl to make a starter hole in the very center of the top of the cork and another on the side of the cork, about halfway between the top of the cork and the place where the cork and dowel meet.

7. Paint the dial in a fancy design. Somewhere in the

Astrolabe

The astrolabe was invented by the Arabians around the first century A.D. At first it was used mainly by astronomers. But about the year 1500, sailors began to use it to help navigate their big new clipper ships. (It's hard to use an astrolabe on small ships because they bounce up and down a lot, and you have to hold an astrolabe steady in order to use it.) You can use an astrolabe to measure the altitude of stars and of other heavenly bodies, such as the sun, and also your own latitude on earth.

What You'll Need

A piece of corrugated cardboard about 7 by 7 inches

Something to use as a pattern to draw a circle with a 6-inch diameter

Something to use as a pattern to draw a circle with a 4-inch diameter

A pencil

A razor knife

An awl or a big nail

A 1/4 by 1-inch hex bolt and a wing nut to fit it

A ruler

A protractor*

A piece of soft wood 5 inches long, about 1/2 inch thick, and 3/4 inch wide

A brace and bit or a hand drill with a drill bit slightly larger than the bolt

Acrylic paints and a brush

A fine-point black permanent marker

3 or 4 flat washers that fit around the bolt

A plastic drinking straw

Scissors

2 long straight pins

A piece of heavy thread or string about 18 inches long

A small lead fishing weight or a small bolt to use as a weight

*Protractors are available wherever school, office, or drafting supplies are sold.

What to Do

1. Make the dial by tracing a 6-inch circle on the piece of cardboard and then cutting it out with the razor knife.

2. Center the pattern for the 4-inch circle on this circle, and trace this smaller circle. See Figure 1.

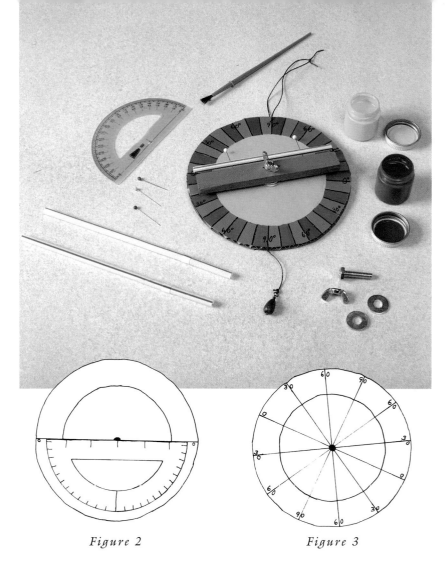

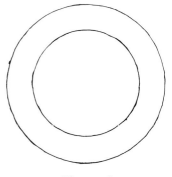

Figure 1

Figure 2

Figure 3

3. Use the awl or nail to poke a hole through the exact center of the circle. Enlarge this hole by turning the awl until the bolt will slide through the hole.

4. Use the ruler to help draw a straight line going from one edge of the cardboard to the other across the center hole. Label both ends of this line "0." Set the protractor on this line, with the center of the protractor over the center of the hole in the middle of the circle. See Figure 2.

5. The protractor is divided into numbered sections, beginning with 0 and going to 90, which is straight up. Mark the place on the outer rim of the

circle straight above 90. Place the ruler across the center hole and touching your 90 mark. Draw a line from edge to edge of the circle, going across the center and touching 90. Label both ends of this line 90.

6. Position the protractor again as you did in Step 5. Mark the places on the outer rim above 60 and also above 30. Draw lines and label the points as you did in Step 1. When you are finished, your dial should look like Figure 3.

7. Next make the sighting arm. Drill a hole in the middle of the wooden stick. This can be tricky, as the hole is going to be big for such a skinny stick. If

the stick splits (and it probably will unless you are very lucky!), simply ask someone to hold it together for you while you continue to drill. Then use carpenter's glue or super glue to glue it back together.

8. Now paint the dial, and use a fine-point marker to number the angles. Also paint all sides and ends of the stick.

9. When the paint has dried completely, assemble the astrolabe. Slide the bolt into the center hole from back to front of the dial. Slip the washers over the bolt and then the piece of wood. Thread the wing nut onto the bolt end, and tighten it to keep the stick from moving around. Push the two pins through the straw about 1 inch in from each end, and then push the pins into the wooden stick. Use the awl to poke a small hole 1/4 inch in from the edge of the cardboard at both 90-degree marks.

10. Tie the fishing weight to one end of a 3-inch piece of string, and tie the other end through one of the small holes on the edge of the dial. Tie a 10-inch piece of string in a loop through the other hole.

11. To use the astrolabe, hang it by the loop from a tree branch or a large nail in the side of a fence or a building so that the instrument hangs freely. To measure the altitude of a star, move the wooden sighting arm so that you can sight the star through the straw. Read the angle that the arm is pointing to. That is the altitude of the star—the number of degrees above the horizon. If you want to measure your own latitude, measure the altitude of the North, or polar, Star. The altitude of the North Star is your latitude if you live in the northern hemisphere.

To measure the altitude of the sun, hold the astrolabe by the loop so that the sun casts a shadow either above or below the stick. Move the stick until the shadow of the stick disappears. (You will still be able to see the shadow of the spacer washers or pipe.) The arm will be pointing directly at the sun, and you can read the dial to learn the altitude of the sun without looking at the sun. Looking directly at the sun can damage your eyes, so NEVER try to sight the sun through the straw. Always use the shadow method for the sun.

136

How Many Stars *Are There?*

Fig. 12

On a clear, dark night, away from city lights, you can see about 4,000 stars in the sky. But actually, those are only a few of the *billions* of stars that we know about.

Our home galaxy, the Milky Way, is an enormous, disc-shaped cluster of stars, dust, and gas. It's so huge that light, which travels 93 million miles from the sun to Earth in about 8 minutes, would take 100,000 *years* to go from one end of the Milky Way to the other.

Our sun is only one of at least 400 billion stars in the Milky Way galaxy. And the Milky Way is only one of billions of galaxies that make up the Universe!

Do Stars Really *Twinkle?*

No. Even if you wish it may and wish it might, no star actually twinkles at night. Stars only *seem* to twinkle—because they're so far away. Our nearest star, after the sun, is 25,000,000,000,000 (25 trillion) miles from Earth!

Stars are so distant that we see their light only as small pinpoints. As the tiny light passes through Earth's thick, ever-moving atmosphere, ripples of warm and cold air are enough to make it quiver and twinkle.

You can create the same effect at home. You'll need a box with a lid (a cereal box is perfect), a nail, a flashlight, and an electric hot plate. Use the nail to punch a bunch of very small holes in one side of the box. Turn on a flashlight, put it in the box, close the lid so that no light escapes, and place the box at one end of a table. Now put the electric hot plate in front of the box, and turn it on. (Be careful—and don't forget to turn off the hot plate as soon as you're done!)

With the room lights off, look at the box from the opposite end of the table through the heated, rising air. The "stars" in your boxy "sky" will twinkle.

If you see a bright spot in the night sky that *doesn't* twinkle, you're probably looking at a planet, not a star. Planets usually don't twinkle, because they're much closer to Earth. In telescopes, we see their light as circles, or discs, rather than pinpoints. More of their light reaches us all at once, so moving air doesn't have much effect.

Where on Earth Are You?

It's a big world out there. Our planet measures nearly 25,000 miles around its middle. There are more than 196,000,000 square miles of land and sea on Planet Earth!

So how do you describe exactly where, in all that space, is a tiny little place such as, say, Paris, France? Or Asheville, North Carolina? Suppose you're in a sinking boat somewhere in the middle of the Pacific Ocean. How do you give your res cuers directions? ("Turn right at Fiji?")

Fortunately, mapmakers long ago invented a system for pinpointing any location in the world. They divided the entire globe into sections using two different kinds of imaginary lines: latitude and longitude.

Latitude tells you how far north or south you are from the equator, which is the imaginary line that runs east and west around the middle of the world. The equator is exactly halfway between the North and South poles. Lines of latitude are also called *parallels*, because they all encircle the earth side by side without crossing. They're numbered starting at the equator, which is called 0 degrees. The North Pole is 90 degrees north latitude, and the South Pole is 90 degrees south latitude. In between the equator and each of the poles, there's one degree of latitude for about every 69 miles (111 kilometers). The distance between one degree of latitude and another is measured in minutes (there are 60 minutes for one degree) and seconds (60 seconds for every minute).

Longitude tells you how far east or west you are from an imaginary vertical line called the *Prime Meridian*. (Other, "ordinary" lines of longitude are simply called *meridians*.) The Prime Meridian runs north and south from the North Pole through Greenwich, England (near London), and then to the South Pole. It divides the globe into two half-circles: the Eastern Hemisphere (everything to the east of the line) and the Western Hemisphere (everything to the west). The place where the two hemispheres meet again, on the opposite side of the world, is called the *International Date Line*.

Meridians are also measured in degrees, minutes, and seconds. The Prime Meridian is the starting point, so it's 0 degrees. The International Date Line is 180 degrees. All the other meridians of longitude fall in between on either the east or west side.

Using latitude and longitude, you can tell anyone exactly where in the world you are. You can also see where one place is compared to another. Some examples are listed below.

Latitude	Longitude	City
48° North	2° East	Paris, France
51° North	0°	London, England
35° North	82° West	Asheville, North Carolina, USA
34° South	151° East	Sydney, Australia
35° North	139° East	Tokyo, Japan
49° North	123° West	Vancouver, B.C., Canada
41° North	12° East	Rome, Italy
22° South	43° West	Rio de Janeiro, Brazil
56° North	38° East	Moscow, Russia
37° North	23° East	Athens, Greece
25° North	80° West	Miami, Florida, USA
64° North	147° West	Fairbanks, Alaska, USA
52° North	13° East	Berlin, Germany
19° North	99° West	Mexico City, Mexico

Star Magnitude Gauge

This device will tell you the brightness—called the magnitude—of a star. The brightest stars are first magnitude stars, the next brightest are second magnitude, and so on. The difference between two levels is roughly 2-1/2 times the brightness of the previous level. All these stars may look about the same to your naked eye.

But with this simple gauge, you can read the different magnitudes of the stars.

What You'll Need

A piece of cardboard or poster board about 10 by 4 inches

A ruler

A pencil

A small coin

A razor knife

An awl or a big nail

Cellophane (Collect this from the outside of packages.)

Cellophane tape

Scissors

Colored plastic tape

Sequins, puffy paint, small buttons, or other small flat objects to make dots

White glue (unless you are using puffy paint)

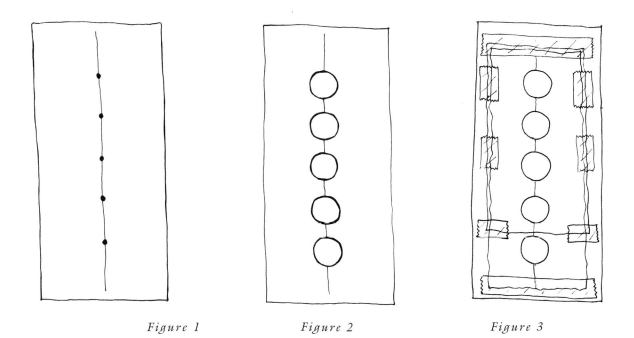

Figure 1   *Figure 2*   *Figure 3*

What to Do

1. Draw a line down the middle of the cardboard going lengthwise. Put a large dot halfway down the line. This should be at about the center of the piece of cardboard. Put two other dots below and two above the center dot, all on the center line and all about 1-1/2 inches from each other. See Figure 1.

2. Place the coin over one of the dots so that the dot is in the center of the coin. Trace around the coin to make a circle that is cut in half by the center line. Do this for each of the five dots.

3. Using the awl or nail, punch little holes along the outline of each circle. Make the holes close together. Then use the razor knife to connect the holes and at the same time cut out the circles. If you are using heavy cardboard or corrugated cardboard, you may have to cut several layers before the entire circle comes

out. When you have finished this step, you should have five holes going down the center of the card. See Figure 2.

4. Tape a piece of cellophane over all five holes. Stretch it tight so there are no wrinkles.

5. Now cut a piece of cellophane big enough to cover four of the holes. Begin with the second hole down, and tape this piece of cellophane over four holes. See Figure 3. Next, cut a piece of cellophane to cover three holes. Begin with the third hole down, and tape this piece over three holes. Then cut a piece of cellophane to cover two holes, and tape this piece over the two bottom holes. Finally, cut a piece of cellophane to cover one hole, and tape this piece over the bottom hole. All five holes should now be covered with cellophane in layers going from one at the top to five at the bottom.

6. Use plastic tape to cover everything on the card except for the holes.

7. Glue sequins, buttons, beads, or other counters next to the holes (or use puffy paint to make dots). Attach your dots in this order: The hole with one layer of cellophane should have five sequins (or whatever you are using) next to it; the hole with two layers should have four; the hole with three layers should have three dots; the hole with four layers should have two dots; and the hole with five layers should have one dot next to it.

8. To use the star magnitude gauge, go outside on a clear night. Look at a star through the one-dot hole (Magnitude 1). If you can't see the star, move to the two-dot hole (Magnitude 2). Keep moving until you can see the star. Whichever hole lets you see the star will tell you roughly the magnitude or brightness of that star.

Cross Staff

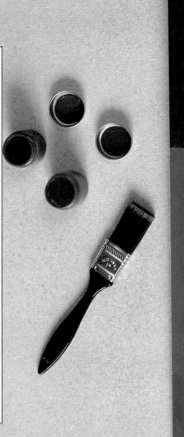

This is one of the oldest navigational instruments. Sailors began using it about the year 1320 to measure the altitude of stars—which allowed them to tell time and find their direction at night. You can easily make your own cross staff and use it to find the altitude of stars, as well as your own latitude.

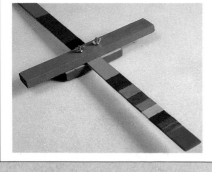

What You'll Need

A piece of wood about 3 feet long by 1-1/2 inches wide by 1/4 inch thick

A piece of wood about 17 inches long by 2 inches wide by 1 inch thick

A pencil

A saw

A ruler

A brace and bit or a hand drill with a drill bit slightly wider than the bolts you will use

2 carriage bolts that are at least 2-1/2 inches long, with wing nuts

Sandpaper

A yardstick

A protractor*

Acrylic paints

A paint brush

A black, fine-tipped permanent marker

*Protractors are available at school, office, or drafting supply stores.

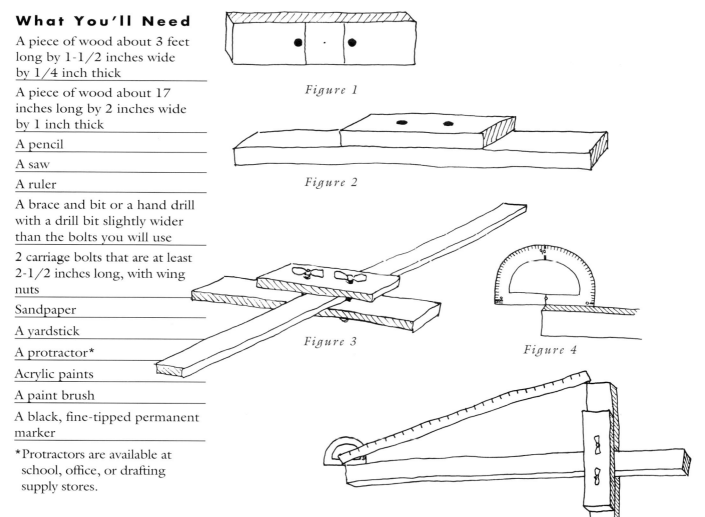

Figure 1

Figure 2

Figure 3

Figure 4

Figure 5

What to Do

1. Saw the 17-inch-long piece of wood into two pieces—one about 5 inches long, and one about 12 inches long.

2. Use the ruler and pencil to mark the center of the 5-inch piece of wood. Lay the 3-foot-long piece of wood crossways over this center mark. Draw a line along each side of the long piece of wood. Remove the long piece of wood, and make two large dots: They should be centered and JUST OUTSIDE each of the two lines you drew. See Figure 1.

3. Drill a hole through the 5-inch piece of wood at each of the two large dots.

4. Center the 12-inch piece of wood under the 5-inch piece. See Figure 2. Stick the pencil down each drilled hole, and mark the wood underneath. Drill holes in the marked spots on this piece of wood, too. Now test the assembly by placing the 3-foot-long piece of wood between the holes in the other two pieces and slipping the bolts through the two pairs of holes. The wood should fit easily between the bolts. Tighten the wing nuts to hold the 3-foot-long piece of wood in position. See Figure 3.

5. If everything fits, you can

mark the angles on the staff. Lay the cross staff on the floor. Loosen the wing nuts, and slide the crosspiece—the two pieces of wood bolted together—down to about 4 inches from one end of the long stick. Place the protractor along the opposite end of the long stick. See Figure 4.

6. You will notice that the protractor has angles marked going from 0 to 90 (straight up) to 180. Place the yardstick from the top of the crosspiece to the end of the long stick over the protractor. Slide the crosspiece (and push the yardstick so that it stays in contact with both cross-

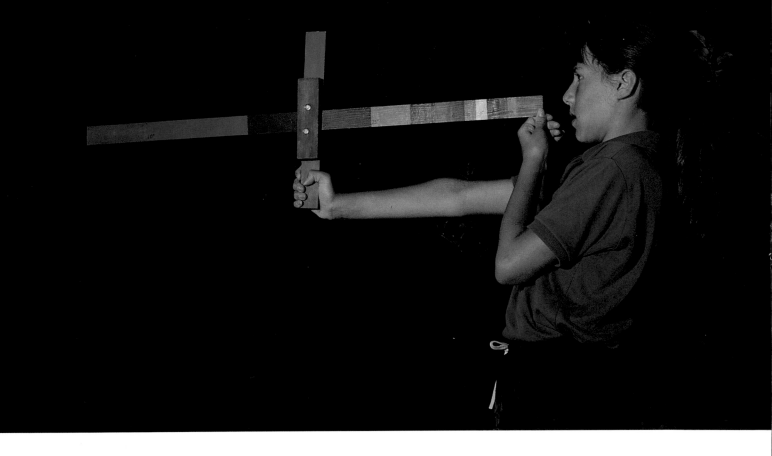

piece and long stick) so that the yardstick lies along the 10-degree line of the protractor. See Figure 5. Draw a line across the flat surface of the long stick, using the side of the crosspiece that is closest to the protractor as a guide. When the crosspiece is in this position, the reading will be 10 degrees.

7. Now mark 15 degrees, following the directions for Step 6. Continue marking every 5 degrees until you come to the end of the long stick. You should be able to get up to 65 or 70 degrees.

8. Take the instrument completely apart to paint it. Paint one color between 0 and 10 degrees, another color between 10 and 15, and so on. After you have painted it, draw over the numbers with black marker so that they can be easily read.

9. When the paint is completely dry, put the cross staff back together.

10. To use your cross staff, go outside at night. Loosen the wing nuts a little so that you can slide the crosspiece. Hold the long piece at eye level, with the higher numbers toward you.

Sight a star along the edge of the wood and the top edge of the crosspiece. Slide the crosspiece until it lines up with the line of sight. Read the number closest to where the crosspiece crosses the long piece of wood. That is the altitude of the star—for example, 30 degrees altitude.

If you want to know your latitude (and you live in the northern hemisphere), find the altitude of the North, or polar, Star. The altitude of the North Star is your latitude.

Is Anybody Out There?

Have you ever gazed up at the stars twinkling in the night sky and wondered if, somewhere out there at that very moment, another creature on another planet was also staring out into space—and wondering?

Most astronomers think that, because there are so many stars that resemble our sun, the chances are good that other life-forms exist on other planets. Some scientists believe that at least 40 billion of the stars in the Milky Way galaxy are about the same age and temperature as our sun. And they think that about 1/10th of those stars (4 billion) could have a planet that, like Earth, is able to support life.

In fact, other life-forms may be trying to contact us right now. So on October 12, 1992, exactly 500 years after Christopher Columbus set sail for the New World, scientists from NASA—the United States' National Aeronautics and Space Administration—launched a special 10-year listening project. Researchers are using the most powerful radio telescopes in the world to search the heavens for alien messages!

A radio telescope works like a TV satellite dish—and looks like one, too, except it's much larger. It collects all the radio waves that strike it, and feeds them to a receiver, where scientists can study the waves for unusual or interesting patterns. The listening-for-aliens project is officially called the High Resolution Microwave Survey. But most star watchers know it as SETI: the Search for Extraterrestrial Intelligence.

In one part of the study, scientists are scanning the entire sky for messages, using radio telescopes in California and Australia. The movable-dish telescopes sweep the heavens in wide figure-eight motions. They can tune into a lot of radio channels at once—up to 32 million—but can detect only fairly strong signals.

Another part of the project, called the Targeted Search, is focusing on what astronomers think are the most promising places to look for intelligent life: the 800 sunlike stars closest to Earth. The radio telescopes for this study can tune in to "only" 10 million channels at once, but they can pick up signals 1,000 times weaker. One of the radio telescopes for this study is the biggest on Earth: a 1,000-foot-wide, dish-shaped antenna set in a jungle valley near Arecibo, Puerto Rico.

Not all scientists believe that alien life exists. What do you think? Are humans alone in the Universe? Or are we just one intelligent life-form among many?

For centuries, we've only been able to stare at the sky and wonder. Maybe soon we'll discover the answer!

METRIC CONVERSION CHART

Although the conversions aren't exact, there are about 2-1/2 centimeters in an inch. So to convert inches to centimeters, just multiply the number of inches by 2.5.

To convert feet to meters, divide the number of feet by 3.25.

INCHES	MILLIMETERS
1/8	3
1/4	6
1/2	13
3/4	19

INCHES	CENTIMETERS
1	2.5
1-1/4	3.2
1-1/2	3.8
1-3/4	4.4
2	5
3	7.5
4	10
5	12.5
6	15
7	17.5
8	20
9	22.5
10	25
11	27.5
12	30
13	32.5
14	35
15	37.5
16	40
17	42.5
18	45
19	47.5
20	50
21	52.5
22	55
23	57.5
24	60
25	62.5
26	65
27	67.5
28	70
29	72.5
30	75

INDEX